C000152805

This book is a special gift

To:

_____

From:

_____

Date:

_____

Message:

_____

_____

Walking
with
the
Saviour

Max Lucado

WALKING WITH THE SAVIOUR
by Max Lucado

Copyright © 1993 by Max Lucado
Quotations from Max Lucado compiled by Karen Hill.
Originally published as an inspirational calendar under
the title *Walking with the Savior* by Max Lucado.

Unless otherwise indicated, all Scripture quotations
are taken from the *Holy Bible,* New Century Version. Copyright ©
1987, 1988, 1991 by Word Publishers, Dallas, Texas 75039.
Used by permission.

© 2000 Christian Art, PO Box 1599,
Vereeniging, 1930, South Africa

Designed by Christian Art

ISBN 1-86852-598-8

Printed in Hong Kong

00 01 02 03 04 05 06 07 08 09 - 10 9 8 7 6 5 4 3 2 1

Walking
with
the
Saviour

JANUARY

CITIZENSHIP IN HEAVEN

"I tell you the truth, whoever hears what I say and believes in the One who sent me has eternal life."
John 5:24

With the coming of another year we are reminded that time is passing. The grains of sand are dripping through the hourglass; sometimes they seem to pass so quickly. That is a frightening thing for those who have no hope. But for those of us whose citizenship is in heaven, it's only good and it's only right.

JANUARY 2

PEACE IN ME

*"I told you these things so that you
can have peace in me. In this world
you will have trouble, but be brave!
I have defeated the world."*
John 16:33

Could you use some peace in your life today? When your life is in turmoil and you wonder if there will ever be another peaceful day for you, open your heart to the God of peace and to Jesus, the Prince of Peace. They will envelop you in a peace that transcends understanding.

JANUARY 3

DWELLING IN THE HIGHLANDS

Jesus has the power of God, by which he has given us everything we need to live and to serve God. We have these things because we know him. Jesus called us by his glory and goodness.
2 Peter 1:3

Jesus has come into our dark hearts and extended a hand – he has broken in from the outside by an act of God and has lifted us back up. Spiritually, we are secure. We're dwelling in the highlands with him.

JANUARY 4

LIFTED UP BY HIS MERCY

*So I bow in prayer before the Father
from whom every family in heaven and
on earth gets its true name. I ask the
Father in his great glory to give you the
power to be strong inwardly through his
Spirit. I pray that Christ will live in your
hearts by faith and that your life will be
strong in love and be built on love.*
Ephesians 3:14-17

Prayer is the recognition that if God had
not engaged himself in our problems, we
would still be lost in the blackness. It is by
his mercy that we have been lifted up.
Prayer is that whole process that reminds
us of who God is and who we are.

FORGIVENESS

*I pray that you and all God's holy
people will have the power to
understand the greatness of Christ's
love – how wide and how long and
how high and how deep that love is.*
Ephesians 3:18

When you forgive someone, you are as
close to God as you will ever be, because
in that forgiveness you are demonstrating
the very heart of God, the merciful King.
If you want to understand God, if you
want to draw closer to him, then forgive
someone today.

SOURCE OF LIGHT
AND STRENGTH

Since you were a child you have known the Holy Scriptures which are able to make you wise. And that wisdom leads to salvation through faith in Christ Jesus.
2 Timothy 3:15

Father, make us aware of how precious your Word is. Bless those who transport your Word to far off places, to people who haven't been able to open your Word. Thank you, Father, for giving us this source of light and strength, and for giving us the opportunity to uncover the jewels waiting to be discovered in your holy pages.

GIFTS OF LOVE

*Lord All-Powerful, happy
are the people who trust you!*
Psalm 84:12

Father, you have expressed toward us
unlimited mercy. The only reason this
world continues is because you have mercy
upon us. Millions of people today are
receiving food for which they'll never give
thanks. We're breathing air that we take
for granted. Somehow, though, you continue to feed us with your mercy and forgiveness. Thank you for the unimaginable gifts
of your love.

JANUARY 8

Equipping You

"He gives strength to those who are tired and more power to those who are weak ... But the people who trust the Lord will become strong again. They will rise up as an eagle in the sky; they will run and not need rest; they will walk and not become tired."
Isaiah 40:29, 31

You get impatient with your own life, trying to master a habit or control a sin — and in your frustration begin to wonder where the power of God is. Be patient. God is using today's difficulties to strengthen you for tomorrow. He is *equipping* you. The God who makes things grow will help you bear fruit.

JANUARY 9

HUMILITY

The Lord is pleased with his people; he saves the humble.
Psalm 149:4

God exalts humility. When God works in our lives, helping us to become humble, he gives us a permanent joy: humility gives us a joy that cannot be taken away.

THE FOUNDATION

"You have not seen Christ, but you still love him. You cannot see him now, but you believe in him. So you are filled with a joy that cannot be explained, a joy full of glory."
1 Peter 1:8

I believe that a carpenter, the Nazarene carpenter with the Galilean accent and calloused hands, was not merely a man, but he was God. That's the foundation upon which you must build. It's the foundation that says, "My sins have been taken care of, my life has a purpose, and death holds no power over me because I believe in the death conqueror."

JANUARY 11

THOSE HANDS

"I leave you peace; my peace I give you ... So don't let your hearts be troubled or afraid."
John 14:27

We serve the God who designed the universe and set our world in motion. But those hands that hung the stars in the heavens also wiped away the tears of the widow and the leper. And they will wipe away your tears as well.

He Simply Waits

*The Lord is not slow in doing
what he promised – the way some people
understand slowness. But God is being
patient with you. He does not want
anyone to be lost, but he wants all
people to change their hearts and lives.*
2 Peter 3:9

It's God's greatest dream for you to go to heaven – his priority is to get you into his kingdom. And yet, though he is sovereign, he never forces his will on any human being – he simply waits on your acknowledgment of him as Lord.

JANUARY 13

GUARD YOUR HEART!

"Do not give the devil a way to defeat you."
Ephesians 4:27

I am terribly concerned as I hear more and more about how people flirt with immorality and how people dance with materialism and how they consider themselves invulnerable to Satan. We are not invulnerable to Satan – he's wise, he's crafty ... and just as God wishes you to spend forever with him in heaven, Satan wishes you to spend eternity separated from God. Guard your heart!

My Help Comes From The Lord

I look up to the hills, but where does my help come from? My help comes from the Lord; who made heaven and earth.
Psalm 121:1-2

Are you discouraged? Are you weary? You've been promised a life of rest. You've been promised eternity. Even in the face of death we should not grow discouraged, but we do. Let your prayer be that God will empower his Word with his Spirit to blow away the clouds of discouragement circling overhead and increase your courage and faith.

ONE DAY AT A TIME

*God, my strength, I will sing
praises to you. God, my defender,
you are the God who loves me.*
Psalm 59:17

Life is too big to be resolved in one day ...
just take the challenges that come your way
one day at a time.

God's Grace

I trust in your love. My heart is happy because you saved me. I sing to the Lord because he has taken care of me.
Psalm 13:5-6

The gospels are like a tapestry, woven together with two incredible points: the immeasurable value of each person and the unimaginable depth of God's grace.

To Catch A Glimpse

As you received Christ Jesus the
Lord, so continue to live in him.
Keep your roots deep in him
and have your lives built on him.
Colossians 2:6-7

In essence, Christianity is nothing more, nothing less than a desire and an effort to see Jesus. That's all it is. We're trying to catch a glimpse of a man, not a program, not a plan, not a system, not a doctrine. We're trying to see a man who called himself the Son of God.

You Formed Me

You made my whole being; you formed me in my mother's body. I praise you because you made me in an amazing and wonderful way. What you have done is wonderful. I know this very well.
Psalm 139:13-14

When you wake up and look in the mirror in the morning, you're seeing God's *poetry*. You may think he's not much of a poet, but when God wove you together, it was not by accident, it was not happenstance, it was not a mistake. You are the result of all the creative energy of an omnipotent, omnipresent, and omniscient God poured into the formation of humanity.

God Loves Me

My God loves me, and he goes in front of me. He will help me defeat my enemies.
Psalm 59:10

Over and over Jesus would do the same thing and tell the same story: He would love Nicodemus, so caught up in false religion, but would hate the false religion; he would love the woman caught in adultery, but condemn the adultery; he would love Zaccheus, so obsessed by his possessions, but hate his materialism. He would love the sinner, but hate the sin.

NOTHING BESIDES YOU

I have no one in heaven but you; I want nothing on earth besides you.
Psalm 73:25

The love of Christ compels us to do what we never thought we could do and go to heights we never thought we could reach. Precious is the name of Jesus!

GOD MEETS OUR NEEDS

Don't say, "I'll pay you back for the wrong you did." Wait for the Lord, and he will make things right.
Proverbs 20:22

Sometimes life doesn't seem fair, does it? Have you ever wondered why good people have to hurt? Why the innocent suffer? Often it seems that those who have been most battered by life seem to understand Jesus best, and his assurance finds its way into the darkest corners of life because, regardless of our circumstances, God meets our needs. By surrendering to him, the ultimate victory is ours.

JANUARY 22

TRULY FREE!

*But I will sing about your strength.
In the morning I will sing about
your love. You are my defender, my
place of safety in times of trouble.*
Psalm 59:16

We have been liberated from our own guilt and our own legalism. We have the freedom to pray and the freedom to love the God of our heart. And we have been forgiven by the only one who could condemn us. We are truly free!

FORGIVE EACH OTHER

Be kind and loving to each other,
and forgive each other just
as God forgave you in Christ.
Ephesians 4:32

Our forgiveness of others is a signal of our awareness of how much God has given us.

Eternal Treasure

*"Don't store treasures for yourselves
here on earth ... But store your treasures
in heaven where they cannot be destroyed
by moths or rust and where thieves cannot
break in and steal them. Your heart
will be where your treasure is."*
Matthew 6:19-21

Father, keep us from being so blinded by possessions that we cannot keep that we would fail to see the eternal treasure we cannot lose.

Before God's Throne

Let us, then, feel very sure that we can come before God's throne where there is grace. There we can receive mercy and grace to help us when we need it.
Hebrews 4:16

In our "bootstrap" society, where you tough it up and do it on your own and take pride in being a rugged individualist, the one thing that seems to escape us is being before God on our knees, being before God aware that we are helpless, and *allowing* him to assist us.

JANUARY 26

ALL THIS IS FROM GOD

*All this is from God. Through
Christ, God made peace between
us and himself, and God gave us the
work of telling everyone about
the peace we can have with him.*
2 Corinthians 5:18

Blessed Lord and God, we come to you,
aware that you have pierced our world.
You became flesh, you dwelled among us,
you saw us in our fallen state, you reached
in and pulled us out. You offered us salvation, you offered us mercy. And we are ever
thankful.

REMIND US

I want to know Christ and the power that raised him from the dead. I want to share in his sufferings and become like him in his death. Then I have hope that I myself will be raised from the dead.
Philippians 3:10-11

Let us ask our Father humbly, yet confidently in the name of Jesus, to remind us of the empty tomb. Let us see the victorious Jesus: the conqueror of the tomb, the one who defied death. And let us be reminded that we, too, will be granted that same victory!

PRAISE THE LORD

*Praise the Lord for the glory of his name;
worship the Lord because he is holy.*
Psalm 29:2

Praise is the highest occupation of any being. What happens when we praise the Father? We reestablish the proper chain of command; we recognize that the King is on the throne and that he has saved his people.

His Gift Of Mercy

I mean that you have been saved by grace through believing. You did not save yourselves; it was a gift from God.
Ephesians 2:8

God forgave us before we even asked it. He extended mercy to us before we even knew we needed it. Why? Because the God of mercy took pity on us – a band of creatures who are incapable of saving themselves without his gift of mercy.

CRY OUT FOR WISDOM

Listen carefully to wisdom; set your mind on understanding. Cry out for wisdom, and beg for understanding. Search for it like silver, and hunt for it like hidden treasure. Then you will understand respect for the Lord, and you will find that you know God.
Proverbs 2:2-5

Do you have a hunger for the Word of God? I challenge you to rediscover the Bible in your own life ... to regain the same hunger and enthusiasm you felt when you first heard the name of Jesus!

JANUARY 31

THE RIVER OF ETERNITY

This is what God told us: God has given us eternal life, and this life is in his Son.
1 John 5:11

Several hundred years before Jesus, Isaiah said that there is one who is chosen; there is one who is promised. He said that something would happen that would convince us that we're not spinning in a whirlpool headed toward nowhere, but we're floating down the river of eternity guided by God.

FEBRUARY

LIVE IN PEACE

*Wish good for those who harm you;
wish them well and do not curse
them. Be happy with those who are
happy, and be sad with those who are
sad. Live in peace with each other.*
Romans 12:14-16

Who are peacemakers? They are the first
ones who take the initiative and *decide* to
extend their hands as olive branches of
peace. If someone has hurt you, it is *your*
responsibility to rebuild the bridge of
relationship.

FEBRUARY 2

JUST AS WE ARE

Now may God himself, the God of peace,
make you pure, belonging only to him.
May your whole self – spirit, soul, and
body – be kept safe and without fault
when our Lord Jesus Christ comes.
1 Thessalonians 5:23

Here we are, Father. We call ourselves your
people, yet we carry the baggage of a week
of concerns. We come to you just as we
are, without trying to hide our mistakes.
Father, mend us and make us better than
we could be alone. Take that which is
broken in our lives and make it stronger
at the broken places. And use that new
strength in your kingdom.

FEBRUARY 3

BE PATIENT

Depend on the Lord; trust him,
and he will take care of you.
Psalm 37:5

Don't hurry God. The problems that we think may drown us today could be the very stepping-stones to greater spiritual strength tomorrow. Throughout Scripture we are reminded to be patient in suffering, in physical distress, in emotional discouragement. The Father will supply your needs. Don't hurry God.

Perfect Communion

*In Christ we can come before God
with freedom and without fear. We
can do this through faith in Christ.*
Ephesians 3:12

Prayer is the most powerful tool in God's
kingdom, because in prayer we are in
perfect communion with God, interceding
with the Father on behalf of his creation.
The majesty of prayer puts us in the relationship God intended to have with man:
perfect communion.

BUILDING BRIDGES

*It is good and pleasant when
God's people live together in peace!*
Psalm 133:1

God of peace, Father of comfort, we pray that your kingdom would come into our hearts and that peace would rule. Teach us what it means to be peacemakers. Help us cultivate peace between others and you – in our neighborhoods, offices, schoolrooms. Teach us the art of building bridges and not walls. We glorify your name, the great God of peace.

SHOW MERCY

"Love your enemies. Do good to those who hate you, bless those who curse you, pray for those who are cruel to you ... Show mercy, just as your Father shows mercy."
Luke 6:27-28, 36

What do you do when people mistreat you or those you love? Does the fire of anger boil within you, with leaping flames consuming your emotions? Or do you reach somewhere, to some source of cool water and pull out a bucket of mercy – to free yourself? Is there any emotion that imprisons the soul more than the unwillingness to forgive? Can you reach for that cool water of forgiveness today?

GOD'S TEACHING

But the truly happy people are those who carefully study God's perfect law that makes people free, and they continue to study it. They do not forget what they heard, but they obey what God's teaching says. Those who do this will be made happy.
James 1:25

If you want to grow in the Word of God, become a person with a chisel and quarry the Word – look, explore, seek. Let the Word become your Word, and you will grow.

THOSE WHO FOLLOW CHRIST

Then people will say, "There really are rewards for doing what is right. There really is a God who judges the world."
Psalm 58:11

Listen to the Christ rather than to the voices of men. Jesus says you can't please men and still be a servant of God. Those who listen and follow Christ will be received into heaven by the pierced hands of the one who knows the freedom of giving up what you cannot own in order to receive what no one can take from you – eternal life.

FEBRUARY 9

SUCH A PRIVILEGE

Yes, it is through Christ we all have the right to come to the Father in one Spirit.
Ephesians 2:18

Father, it's with earnestness that we come to you, asking you to open our hearts and let the drafts of heaven come inside. Thank you for the great blessing you've given us in allowing us to come to you in prayer and stand in your presence. Holy is your name that you would allow us to have such a privilege.

An Unquenchable Belief

This is how God showed his love to us: He sent his one and only Son into the world so that we could have life through him.
1 John 4:9

The fire that lit the boiler of the New Testament church was an unquenchable belief that if Jesus had been only a man, he would have stayed in the tomb. They couldn't stay silent about the fact that the one they saw hung on a cross walked again on the earth and appeared to 500 people. I wonder if sometimes we stay silent because we've forgotten the one who was on that cross.

REGATHER STRENGTH

God rested from all his works.
Hebrews 4:4

Sometimes the most godly thing we can do for ourselves is to go to sleep. Sometimes the most godly thing we can do for our family and friends is to take a break and regather our strength.

REMEMBER THE LORD

*"I will be with you always,
even until the end of this age."*
Matthew 28:20

Remember the Lord. Remember who is in control. Remember his goodness in the past. Remember God's closeness in the present. Remember his power for the future.

RESIST DISCOURAGEMENT

The sun cannot hurt you during the day, and the moon cannot hurt you at night. The Lord will protect you from all dangers; he will guard your life.
Psalm 121:6-7

Resist discouragement. Don't let it control you. Nobody can take away from you your capacity to make a decision regarding discouragement. You have the power to determine not to let discouraging circumstances engulf you. As Christians who can call on the power of God, we have every reason not to feel discouraged.

HIS VERY BEST!

*This is what real love is: It is not
our love for God; it is God's love
for us in sending his Son to be
the way to take away our sins.*
1 John 4:10

I hope you receive a rose or a special card
from that special person today. If you didn't
and don't expect to, remember that the one
who loves you most has already sent you
his very best!

BRING YOUR FEARS TO ME

Don't be afraid of what they fear;
do not dread those things.
1 Peter 3:14

Jesus is not afraid of the things that cause us fear. He never said, "Don't bring your fears to me; I'm too busy." Instead, he said, "I'm not afraid of the things that cause you fear. Bring your fears to me."

LISTENING TO
THE WRONG VOICE

My dear friends, many false prophets have gone out into the world. So do not believe every spirit, but test the spirits to see if they are from God.
1 John 4:1

Have you ever listened to the wrong voice? Have you ever taken the wrong advice? Oftentimes the cause of a crisis in our life is that we listen to the wrong voice. To whose voice will you listen today?

BUILD ONLY ON FAITH

*The people who obey God's command
live in God, and God lives in them.
We know that God lives in us
because of the Spirit God gave us.*
1 John 3:24

Don't build your house on a career. Don't build your house on a thrill. Don't build your house on a talent. Don't build your house on one solitary earthly relationship. Don't pursue things that don't last. Build your house on the only thing that can last: faith.

A New Day

*"With the loving mercy of our God, a
new day from heaven will dawn upon us."*
Luke 1:78

Perhaps the heaviest burden we try to carry
is the burden of mistakes, failures. What
do you do with your failures? Do you carry
them around with you? We can't carry our
mistakes alone – somebody has to help us
carry them. God doesn't want you burdened with past failures. He wants you
freed of them, and he's the only one who
can give you that freedom.

THE SOURCE OF STRENGTH

*Strengthen yourselves so that you will
live here on earth doing what God
wants, not the evil things people want.*
1 Peter 4:2

The most powerful life is the most simple
life. The most powerful life is the life that
knows where it's going, that knows where
the source of strength is, and the life that
stays free of clutter and happenstance and
hurriedness.

LOVE AND TRUTH

Love and truth belong to God's people;
goodness and peace will be theirs.
Psalm 85:10

Peace is never sought at the expense of truth. God never calls us into a relationship with him just to have a relationship. He sets truth in front of us and says, "Agree to that truth and then we can have a relationship."

MAKE PRAYER A PRIORITY

Continue praying, keeping alert,
and always thanking God.
Colossians 4:2

Father, when you were on earth, you prayed. You prayed in the morning, you prayed at night, you prayed alone, you prayed with people. In your hours of distress you retreated into times of prayer. In your hours of joy you lifted your heart and hands to the Father in prayer. Help us to be more like you in this way ... help us to make prayer a priority in our daily lives.

GOD IS MERCIFUL

*God, be merciful to me because you are
loving. Because you are always ready
to be merciful, wipe out all my wrongs.*
Psalm 51:1

We have nothing to offer God in exchange
for what he has given us. It's not that we
don't have any value; it's just that we don't
have any right to request the forgiveness
we so desperately need and which he is so
willing to share.

TOTAL SURRENDER

But if we confess our sins, he will forgive our sins, because we can trust God to do what is right. He will cleanse us from all the wrongs we have done.
1 John 1:9

We don't like to recognize our ruin, but that's where Jesus begins. Once we're honest with ourselves about who we are, then God can begin to remold our hearts ... total surrender.

THE WORDS PIERCE

*God's word is alive and working
and is sharper than a double-edged
sword. It cuts all the way into us,
where the soul and the spirit are
joined, to the center of our joints
and bones. And it judges the
thoughts and feelings in our hearts.*
Hebrews 4:12

We go to the Word of God for comfort, and when we do, the words pierce like a surgeon's scalpel, both cutting and healing. The Word of God cuts to the very place where thoughts and attitudes come together, at the juncture of soul and spirit, providing a healing that can be obtained in no other way on earth.

CALL TO HIM

*I love the Lord, because he listens
to my prayers for help. He paid
attention to me, so I will call
to him for help as long as I live.*
Psalm 116:1-2

God is an exalted friend, a holy Father, and an elevated King. How do we approach him — as king, as father, or as friend? The answer: yes!

GET RID OF THE RUBBLE

The Lord defends those who suffer;
he defends them in times of trouble.
Psalm 9:9

Does the rubble of your life take you off course and cause frustration? Get rid of the rubble – organize your day, decide where to start and where to finish. Sometimes we think that being a Christian means saying yes to every request that comes our way. Sometimes you are being more faithful by being disciplined and knowing where to use your gifts. Put your strengths on strengths.

FEBRUARY 27

IF ONLY WE'LL WAIT

The Lord does what is right, and he loves justice, so honest people will see his face.
Psalm 11:7

Father, nothing is louder than the silence of our God. But Father, forgive us for the times we've interpreted your silence as a lack of love. Give us patience, for we know you'll answer, Father, if only we'll wait.

Set On The Course

*Trust the Lord with all your heart,
and don't depend on your own understanding. Remember the Lord in all
you do, and he will give you success.*
Proverbs 3:5-6

We know that someday our heavenly Father is going to take all those who follow him into eternal happiness. It's to that day that we look. It's upon our hope and confidence that he will return that we stand. Our prayer should be that our Father will help us make decisions that will set us on the course of eternal life.

It's Not Fair

Those who are honest will live in the land, and those who are innocent will remain in it. But the wicked will be removed from the land, and the unfaithful will be thrown out of it.
Proverbs 2:21-22

When we look at the world around us, sometimes it's difficult to understand the unfairness of life. It's not fair that the young should suffer. It's not fair that the innocent should go hungry. But nor is it fair that a God would have to come to earth and hang on his own cross to protect us from the evil one. It's not fair ... but that's *love*. And that's God.

MARCH

People Of God

This service you do not only helps the needs of God's people, it also brings many more thanks to God. It is a proof of our faith. Many people will praise God because you obey the Good News of Christ – the gospel you say you believe – and because you freely share with them and with all others.
2 Corinthians 9:12-13

There is a special place in our hearts for people who have names we cannot even pronounce and speak languages we cannot speak and live in places we'll never visit – who are, as we are, people of God.

THE TRUE GRACE

This is the true grace of God.
Stand strong in that grace.
1 Peter 5:12

We're not perfect, Father, but we are yours. We're not what we should be, but we do claim your salvation and your grace. We ask you to make us every day more and more into the image of Jesus Christ. We stand amazed that you would have such mercy upon us to forgive us time and time again. Thank you for the immeasurable depth of your grace.

A Seed Of Peace

*"I am the Lord your God, who teaches
you to do what is good, who leads
you in the way you should go. If you
had obeyed me, you would have
had peace like a full-flowing river."*
Isaiah 48:17-18

Perhaps the seeds you sow in your areas of conflict won't reach maturity tomorrow, next week or even for a generation. Does that mean you shouldn't sow the seeds *immediately*? Never underestimate the power of a seed of peace: the power of a kind word, a seed of apology, a phone call, an explanation. This is the way we serve a God of peace.

WHEN GOD'S
PEOPLE INTERCEDE

*When a believing person
prays, great things happen.*
James 5:16

God's power is unleashed when God's
people intercede.

THOSE WHO WIN THE VICTORY

"Those who win the victory will sit with me on my throne in the same way that I won the victory and sat down with my Father on his throne."
Revelation 3:21

I believe that praise and prayer develop us for what we will do when we arrive in heaven. What's your picture of what you'll be doing there – sitting on a cloud? Polishing your halo? Playing your harp? That's not what you're going to be doing. You're going to be involved in the ongoing process of co-reigning with God.

POSSIBLE TO FORGIVE

Don't judge other people, and you will not be judged. Don't accuse others of being guilty, and you will not be accused of being guilty. Forgive, and you will be forgiven.
Luke 6:37

Go back to the Cross and see how God through the Cross forgives us: that gives us strength to forgive each other. We have a mandate to forgive, a liberating concept that says you have a choice. You don't have to live with anger or resentment – you can get rid of it. It *is* possible to forgive – through prayer and the Holy Spirit, it *is* possible!

THE TEACHING OF CHRIST

Let the teaching of Christ live in you richly. Use all wisdom to teach and instruct each other by singing psalms, hymns, and spiritual songs with thankfulness in your hearts to God.
Colossians 3:16

The purpose of the Christian life is not to memorize the Bible just for the sake of memorizing the text. The Bible was provided for us as a vehicle to carry us so that we might be able to see Jesus Christ.

THY KINGDOM COME

So that every knee will bow to the name of Jesus – everyone in heaven, on earth, and under the earth. And everyone will confess that Jesus Christ is Lord and bring glory to God the Father.
Philippians 2:10-11

Thy kingdom come, Lord. Let your kingdom live in the hearts of people, let your kingdom live in society, let the church be strong, and let your kingdom come eternally.

WORTHY OF PRAISE

I will praise the Lord at all times;
his praise is always on my lips. My
whole being praises the Lord.
Psalm 34:1-2

We should serve God even if there is darkness enveloping our life and even if we don't understand what's happening ... even when the circumstances of our life don't make sense: Because he is worthy of praise, *because he is God.*

DEEP GRACE

*Where can I go to get away from your
Spirit? Where can I run from you? If I
go up to the heavens, you are there. If I
lie down in the grave, you are there.*
Psalm 139:7-8

Always remember that Jesus says, "My
grace is deeper than your sins."

HIS LOST SHEEP

Anyone who brings a sinner back from the wrong way will save that sinner's soul from death and will cause many sins to be forgiven.
James 5:20

I wonder if Jesus doesn't muster up a slight smile as he sees his lost sheep come straggling into the fold – the beaten, broken, dirty sheep who stands at the door looking up at the Shepherd asking, "Can I come in? I don't deserve it, but is there room in your kingdom for one more?" The Shepherd looks down at the sheep and says, "Come in, this is your home."

THE ONE CALLED JESUS

Those who preached the Good News to you told you those things with the help of the Holy Spirit who was sent from heaven – things into which angels desire to look.
1 Peter 1:12

Of all the unusual beginnings, there is none more unusual than that of Christianity. The church of our Lord was begun by a group of reluctant followers in a second-story room in Jerusalem. They were timid followers, hesitant soldiers, speechless messengers. They didn't know what to do; they didn't know what to say; but they knew they could not forget the one called Jesus.

MARCH 13

GOD'S COMPASS

*"Make them ready for your service through
your truth; your teaching is truth."*
John 17:17

Just as a navigator can't find his destination without a compass, we can't find peace without God's compass – the Word of Truth.

THE MINISTRY OF PRAYER

Pray continually, and give thanks whatever happens. That is what God wants for you in Christ Jesus.
1 Thessalonians 5:17-18

We should be people of great prayer. We should be prayer warriors. We should be people who use the ministry of prayer to its fullest capacity. The highest and greatest calling of Christians is the ministry of prayer.

GREAT MERCY

God's mercy is great, and he loved us very much. Though we were spiritually dead because of the things we did against God, he gave us new life with Christ. You have been saved by God's grace.
Ephesians 2:4-5

The first step toward forgiveness is to see the other person as a human being, not as a source of hurt. That's how God treated us with mercy – he became one of us, he felt as we feel, he understood our frustrations. And as a result, when he hung on the cross, he could look at those crucifying him and ask God to forgive them.

THE RIGHT FOUNDATION

"Those who want to do right
more than anything else are happy,
because God will fully satisfy them."
Matthew 5:6

The Beatitudes are not suggestions, good ideas, theories for a positive mental attitude – they are the rules for right living. Those that hear them and obey them are building on the right foundation.

Do You Worry?

*All living things look to you for
food, and you give it to them at
the right time. You open your
hand, and you satisfy all living things.*
Psalm 145:15-16

The word *worry* comes from a word that
means "to divide." When you worry, you
divide your energy. Do you worry? I worry
about you if you don't worry! All of us
worry, but we shouldn't. Jesus commands
us half a dozen times, "Do not worry."
When we worry about a situation, the problem gets us instead of us getting it.

To The Lamb Be Praise

"Then I heard all creatures in heaven and on earth and under the earth and in the sea saying: 'To the One who sits on the throne and to the Lamb be praise and honor and glory and power forever and ever.'"
Revelation 5:13

The whole purpose of coming before the King is to praise him, to live in recognition of his splendor. Praise – lifting up our heart and hands, exulting with our voices, singing his praises – is the occupation of those who dwell in the kingdom.

Trust In The Lord

God, I look to you for
help. I trust in you, Lord.
Psalm 141:8

Don't put your hope into things that can change — relationships, money, talents, beauty, even health. Set your sights on the one thing that can never change: trust in your heavenly Father.

Sharing God's Glory

Since we have been made right with God by our faith, we have peace with God. This happened through our Lord Jesus Christ, who has brought us into that blessing of God's grace that we now enjoy. And we are happy because of the hope we have of sharing God's glory.
Romans 5:1-2

When we look at the cross, we feel only gratitude. We thank you, Father, that on the cross you provided forgiveness for our sins, purpose for our life, and an answer for our death. We believe that the tomb couldn't hold you in and that death couldn't keep you down. We believe that when we speak to you, Father, we are addressing the death conqueror.

Follow The Teachings

Everything that was written in the past was written to teach us. The Scriptures give us patience and encouragement so that we can have hope.
Romans 15:4

Your life came with an owner's manual — if you follow the teachings in it, you will be fully equipped and your life will operate much more smoothly.

Fully United In Prayer

"When you are praying, if you are angry with someone, forgive him so that your Father in heaven will also forgive your sins."
Mark 11:25

Isn't it presumptuous to come to the throne of grace if we haven't been gracious to the people in our life? How can we approach a God of mercy if we ourselves have hearts full of bitterness or anger? We must take care of relationship problems – make up with a spouse, get along with fellow church members, love our neighbors – then we will be fully united in prayer with the Father.

RECOGNIZE YOUR PRIZE

*I pray also that you will have greater
understanding in your heart so you
will know the hope to which he has
called us and that you will know how
rich and glorious are the blessings
God has promised his holy people.*
Ephesians 1:18

Jesus says the way to deal with your
problems is to recognize your prize. You
see, if we have a prize that's great enough,
our problems become small. There will be
problems on this earth, but there will be a
place where you'll be saved if you'll endure.

Assured Of Victory

Live such good lives that they will see the good things you do and will give glory to God on the day when Christ comes again.
1 Peter 2:12

If you have no faith in the future, then you have no power in the present. If you have no faith in the life beyond this life, then your present life is going to be powerless. But if you believe in the future and are assured of victory, then there should be a dance in your step and a smile on your face.

Pray In The Spirit

*Pray in the Spirit at all times with
all kinds of prayers, asking for everything
you need. To do this you must
always be ready and never give up.
Always pray for all God's people.*
Ephesians 6:18

I would like to encourage you, admonish
you to make a decision to pray more and
to set up some specific plans to support that
decision. Will you determine in your heart
to pray more? Will you start a prayer group
in your home? Pray continually – live in a
spirit of prayer.

A Savior Who Came Down

For this reason Jesus had to be made like his brothers in every way so he could be their merciful and faithful high priest in service to God.
Hebrews 2:17

Our God is not aloof – he's not so far above us that he can't see and understand our problems. Jesus isn't a God who stayed on the mountaintop – he's a Savior who came down and lived and worked with the people. Everywhere he went, the crowds followed, drawn together by the magnet that was – and is – the Savior.

GOD'S TENDERNESS

He takes care of his people like a
shepherd. He gathers them like lambs
in his arms and carries them close to him.
Isaiah 40:11

We have been touched by God's tenderness – all the tenderness of a gentle father. He doesn't come quarrelling and wrangling and forcing his way into anyone's heart. He comes into our hearts like a gentle lamb, not a roaring lion.

You Have Won!

The Lord is not slow in doing what he promised
— the way some people understand slowness.
But God is being patient with you. He does
not want anyone to be lost, but he wants
all people to change their hearts and lives.
2 Peter 3:9

What is unique about the kingdom of God is that you are assured of victory. You have won! You are assured that you will someday stand before the face of God and see the King of kings. You are assured that someday you will enter a world where there will be no more pain, no more tears, no more sorrow.

PEACEMAKERS

*"Those who work to bring peace are happy,
because God will call them his children."*
Matthew 5:9

Make us, O God, into your peacemakers.
Give us courage as we stand on fields of
daily conflict. Let us be tools of reconcilia-
tion; let us be ambassadors of love; let us
be as you are – peacemakers, that we may
be called sons of God.

You Know Everything

You know when I sit down and when I get up. You know my thoughts before I think them. You know where I go and where I lie down. You know thoroughly everything I do.
Psalm 139:2-3

Perhaps the reason that God doesn't always give us the answer to the *whys* of our existence is that he knows we haven't got the capacity to understand the answer. In learning to depend on God, we must accept that we may not know all the answers, but we know *who* knows the answers.

Your Hope Will Overflow

I pray that the God who gives hope will fill you with much joy and peace while you trust in him. Then your hope will overflow by the power of the Holy Spirit.
Romans 15:13

I've noticed that those who serve God most joyfully are the ones who know him most personally. Those who are quickest to speak about Jesus are those who realize how great has been their own redemption.

APRIL

APRIL 1

THAT SWEET SURPRISE

This promise is for you, for your children, and for all who are far away. It is for everyone the Lord our God calls to himself.
Acts 2:39

Holy Father, thank you for the sweet surprise of Easter morning. We are thankful that when you arose from your sleep of death, you didn't go immediately to heaven, but instead you went and visited people. This visit of love reminds us that it was for *people* that you died. We praise your name for that sweet surprise.

The Most Immeasurable Gift

This is how we know what real love is:
Jesus gave his life for us. So we should give
our lives for our brothers and sisters.
1 John 3:16

Amidst all the people at the crucifixion scene there is one person with whom all of us can identify. We can all relate to the crucified crook. All of us hang on the cross beside Jesus. All of us have made the most unimaginable request. And all of us who are in the body of Christ have received the most unimaginable and immeasurable gift that we could ever receive – salvation!

APRIL 3

Source Of Energy

I am the resurrection and the life. Those who believe in me will have life even if they die.
John 11:25

Each statement made by Jesus on the cross is like a post that we see sometimes on the side of the road that reads Power Line Buried Here – and if you dig down, sure enough, you're going to strike power. Those words of Christ are a source of energy into which all of us can tap.

APRIL 4

THE CROSS OF JESUS

Through the cross of Jesus my world was crucified, and I died to the world.
Galatians 6:14

It wasn't the Romans who nailed Jesus to the cross. It wasn't the Jewish religion that took him up the hill of Calvary. It wasn't spikes that held Jesus to the cross. What held him to that cross was his conviction that it was necessary that he become sin — that he who is pure become sin and that the wrath of God be poured down, not upon the creation, but upon the Creator.

THE DIVINE RELATIONSHIP

*But dear friends, use your most
holy faith to build yourselves up,
praying in the Holy Spirit.*
Jude verse 20

When Jesus talks about prayer, he doesn't present it as an arduous task, he doesn't describe it as a requirement, he doesn't say that it's something you do beautifully so that some divine audience will throw flowers to you. That's not what prayer is. It's the divine relationship that allows us to stand before God and express the deepest concerns of our hearts.

WE ARE SET FREE

In Christ we are set free by the blood of his death, and so we have forgiveness of sins. How rich is God's grace, which he has given to us so fully and freely.
Ephesians 1:7

When Jesus told us to pray for forgiveness of our debts as we forgive our own debtors, he knew who would be the one to pay the debt. As he would hang on the cross he would say, "It is finished" ... *the debt is paid!*

THE GRACE OF GOD

Christ ended the law so that everyone who believes in him may be right with God.
Romans 10:4

What is the grace of God? The grace of God says you serve God *because* you're saved, not in order to *be* saved. You love people *because* you're saved, and not in order to *be* saved. You're not trying to keep a legalistic system, you're responding to a system of love and peace.

APRIL 8

THE SURPRISE PARTY

*Mary Magdalene went and said to
the followers, "I saw the Lord!"*
John 20:18

If you like surprises, you should like the
Bible, because God is the God of surprises.
If you like parties, you should like the Bible
because God is the God of parties. If you
like them both, you should like the story
of the surprise party that God gives Mary
when she approaches the tomb.

Simply Because

So you do not belong to yourselves, because you were bought by God for a price.
1 Corinthians 6:19-20

Our value is inherent – it's not based on the Ph.D. after our name or the amount of money in our bank account. We have value simply because we *are*. In the eyes of God, every human has value simply because he is the creation of the almighty God.

YOUR GIFT

"I am the light of the world. The person who follows me will never live in darkness but will have the light that gives life."
John 8:12

An itinerant preacher from Nazareth can do something for the hurt that is in your heart. Maybe you're trying to rebuild an estranged relationship ... Maybe you've been trying to find God for longer than you can remember. There was something about this Nazarene preacher that made people cluster around him like he was God's gift to humanity. He is your gift as well.

Asking Why

No one knows the thoughts of
God except the Spirit of God.
1 Corinthians 2:11

A misconception people have in dealing with life's troubles is that it's wrong to ask why – that a Christian simply accepts and never questions. Abraham, Moses and David all interceded and struggled to understand God. But the lives of these men model for us a total reliance on God, even in the midst of questioning.

APRIL 12

GOD IS LIGHT

*God is light, and in him
there is no darkness at all.*
1 John 1:5

Lord, let us not pretend to be something we're not. You know us early in the morning; you know us late at night. You know us when we're weak; you know us when we're strong. Father, remind us that you still care and that you still love us.

Free Indeed

Don't depend on your own wisdom.
Respect the Lord and refuse to do wrong.
Proverbs 3:7

Holy God and Father in heaven, we come to you, aware that it's not easy to hear your voice amidst the manifold voices of the world. Help us realize that you have truly set us free – free from the lures of status and materialism and peer pressure. Help us remember your promise that when the Son sets us free, we are free indeed.

THE VOICE OF TRUTH

Let us look only to Jesus, the One who began our faith and who makes it perfect.
Hebrews 12:2

The Christian is the one who seeks to discern the voice of God amidst the many voices that come our way. One of the greatest challenges that we have is to learn to hear the voice of truth.

An Anchor For The Soul

*We have this hope as an anchor
for the soul, sure and strong.*
Hebrews 6:19

Nothing and no one can take away God's promise to forgive your sins. Nothing and no one can take away your victory over death. Hold on to your hope, for it is the anchor of your soul.

SHINE LIKE STARS

"The wise people will shine like the brightness of the sky. Those who teach others to live right will shine like stars forever and ever."
Daniel 12:3

Do you ever get tired or bored with your work? Christ says turn your work into a ministry – don't let it be just a vocation. Reach out to people. Let your time at work be a source of joy and encouragement to others, and you'll find greater personal joy and satisfaction as well.

THE BEAUTY OF PRAYER

*Those who know the Lord
trust him, because he will not
leave those who come to him.*
Psalm 9:10

The beauty of prayer is that anyone can pray. You don't have to be a certain age, you don't have to have wealth, you don't have to have a certain talent – all you have to have is a stubborn faith and willingness to intercede.

The First Great Gift

But grow in the grace and knowledge
of our Lord and Savior Jesus Christ.
Glory be to him now and forever! Amen.
2 Peter 3:18

The first great gift God gives his children is his grace. It is a very individually tailored and given gift. Grace is the gift of God's riches: the peace of God, the love of God, the hope of God. We are heirs of God, but at Christ's expense.

An Unusual Guest List

And after you suffer for a short time, God, who gives all grace, will make everything right. He will make you strong and support you and keep you from falling. He called you to share in his glory in Christ, a glory that will continue forever.
1 Peter 5:10

Is there anything that causes you not to have the rest of the Spirit that you need? Jesus issues an invitation to an unusual guest list: those who are tired and over-worked, burdened down. Maybe you could put your name on that guest list.

MADE ALIVE IN THE SPIRIT

Christ himself suffered for sins once. He was not guilty, but he suffered for those who are guilty to bring you to God. His body was killed, but he was made alive in the spirit.
1 Peter 3:18

When the one who knew no sin became sin for us, when the sinless one was covered with all the sins of all the world, God didn't call his army of angels to save him. He didn't, because he knew he would rather give up his Son than give up on us.

THAT PRECIOUS BOOK

*I will follow your rules forever,
because they make me happy.*
Psalm 119:111

Father, we're amazed at how practical your Bible is. Who would have thought that daily help could be found in a book so old. Every time we open it we find it's not old at all. Help us to look for your guidance in that precious book.

APRIL 22

HOLY FREEDOM

*Grace and peace be given to you
more and more, because you truly
know God and Jesus our Lord.*
2 Peter 1:2

Father, help us renew our commitment to
you, to release everything and to be owned
and possessed by you. We long to submit
ourselves to you so that we might know
the holy freedom available to us only
through your grace.

Enough Faith

*"Why are you afraid? You
don't have enough faith."*
Matthew 8:26

Father, as you stilled the storm on the Sea of Galilee, will you still the storms that rage within our hearts? Will you calm the whirling winds of fear and hurt that threaten our faith? Will you, Father, draw us ever closer to you?

APRIL 24

FACE TO FACE

Whoever says that he lives in
God must live as Jesus lived.
1 John 2:6

The apostle Paul gives us the pure motive for Christian service. If Paul were here, he'd call us to stand in front of Christ day after day, knowing that the longer we stand face to face with Jesus, the more dynamic our personal life is going to become.

Say So!

*Anyone who speaks should speak
words from God. Anyone who serves
should serve with the strength God gives
so that in everything God will be praised
through Jesus Christ. Power and glory
belong to him forever and ever. Amen.*
1 Peter 4:11

The psalmist David would tell us that those who have been redeemed will say so! If we're not saying so, perhaps it's because we've forgotten what it is like to be redeemed. Let the redeemed of the earth say so!

THE ONLY HONEST RESPONSE

*"So go and make followers
of all people in the world."*
Matthew 28:19

The only honest response to forgiveness is to speak about it. The only honest response to God's grace is then to share it with others. Any other response is far too timid.

TEARS LIKE A FLOOD

*He was sorry he had made
human beings on the earth, and
his heart was filled with pain.*
Genesis 6:6

Once we see how much God cares for his people, then we begin to see how much his heart must have broken when the hand of man reached out and took the goblet of sin offered by Satan. Because God is perfect, he cannot dwell with a sinful being. He must have wept so much the tears were like a flood and showered the creation.

Sharing The News

*They praised God and were liked
by all the people. Every day the
Lord added those who were being
saved to the group of believers.*
Acts 2:47

There were promises broken at the gate of Gethsemane, and yet, when the disciples fled, they took with them a heart-stopping memory of a man called Jesus. And try as they might, they could not forget him. The beauty of the story is that they spent the rest of their lives sharing the news of salvation.

DEAL WITH IT BOLDLY

*You can trust God, who will
not permit you to be tempted
more than you can stand.*
1 Corinthians 10:13

When you think of the temptation with which you struggle most in your life, you can deal with it boldly. You can have the confidence that God has given you a spirit of self-discipline. It's up to you to tap into that gift.

THE LORD IS KING

The Lord is King forever and ever.
Psalm 10:16

Is there a vacant spot in your heart where there should reside a Savior who died and was resurrected? Do you still have the passion for Jesus that you did years ago? Do you still have the love for the Word that you once did?

MAY

MAY 1

Renew Your Vision

*"Listen! I am coming soon! I will bring
my reward with me, and I will repay
each one of you for what you have done."*
Revelation 22:12

Father, how holy and great is your promise.
You've been so good to us, but somehow,
Father, we find things about which to
complain even though we've been given
life eternal. Renew our vision; help us to
see heaven. Help us to be busy about the
right business – the business of serving you.

No One Is Useless To God

*God does not see the same way people
see. People look at the outside of a
person, but the Lord looks at the heart.*
1 Samuel 16:7

No one is useless to God. No one, at any
point in his life, is useless to God – not a
little child, not the unattractive, not the
clumsy, not the tired, not the discouraged.
God uses his children.

HOW JESUS MUST FEEL

*Then the whole town went out to
see Jesus. When they saw him, they
begged him to leave their area.*
Matthew 8:34

After Jesus cast out the demons, the towns-
people were frightened and asked him to
leave. We don't know what Jesus felt, but
we can imagine what he felt. If you've ever
tried to help somebody and they did not
understand your help, maybe you understand how Jesus felt that day. Perhaps you
can even understand how Jesus must feel
when we reject the one who came to save
us.

WE ARE WAITING

But God made a promise to us, and
we are waiting for a new heaven and
a new earth where goodness lives.
2 Peter 3:13

Father, we know that someday you're going to take all of your followers into eternal happiness. And it is to that day, Father, that we look. And it is upon our hope and confidence that you will return, that we stand.

THE IMPORTANCE OF A FRIEND

*Whoever loves a brother or sister
lives in the light and will not cause
anyone to stumble in his faith.*
1 John 2:10

We know the importance of a friend. All of us need friends, don't we? Whether or not you are friendly could determine whether or not someone hears about Jesus Christ. Your handshake, your warmth, your walk, your friendliness could make the difference in someone's life.

Invite Him In

*My dear friends, if our hearts do not
make us feel guilty, we can come
without fear into God's presence.*
1 John 3:21

Run to Jesus. Jesus wants you to go to him. He wants to become the most important person in your life, the greatest love you'll ever know. He wants you to love him so much that there's no room in your heart and in your life for sin. Invite him to take up residence in your heart.

HAVE COURAGE

*Be alert. Continue strong in the
faith. Have courage, and be strong.*
1 Corinthians 16:13

We don't look like we're afraid, Father –
calm on the outside. But Father, we have
our hidden fears. You know them. We're
afraid of being alone. We're afraid of being
jobless. We're afraid of pain. Father, we
offer these fears to you, and ask you to give
us more courage as we look at you, the
One who knows no fear.

MAY 8

You Were Chosen

*But you are a chosen people, royal priests,
a holy nation, a people for God's own
possession. You were chosen to tell about
the wonderful acts of God, who called you
out of darkness into his wonderful light.*
1 Peter 2:9

As Christians, we symbolize the belief that
Jesus is the Son of God. Perhaps for some
that belief is hidden or almost forgotten.
And yet, for many, that belief is vibrant
and fruitful. Whatever the condition of our
belief, may God daily show us Jesus and
him only. May we constantly see our
redemption and then in turn proclaim it.
How great and sweet is the name of Jesus!

FOOLING OURSELVES

So if we say we have fellowship with God, but we continue living in darkness, we are liars and do not follow the truth ... If we say we have no sin, we are fooling ourselves, and the truth is not in us.
1 John 1:6, 8

We Western-culture-type folks like to deal with things we can see and hold, but when we talk about something from another source, we're uneasy. When something doesn't fit our mentality, we give it a new paradigm – instead of calling evil "Satan", we call evil "the lack of welfare" or "the lack of education." If we can blame Satan's fruits on heredity or heritage, he doesn't seem so mean.

I Call You Friends

I no longer call you servants, because a servant does not know what his master is doing. But I call you friends, because I have made known to you everything I heard from my Father.
John 15:15

Jesus described for his followers what he came to do. He came to build a relationship with people. He came to take away enmity, to take away the strife, to take away the isolation that existed between God and man. Once he bridged that, once he overcame that, he said, "I will call you friends."

GOD'S MERCY

At one time, you were not a people,
but now you are God's people. In the
past you had never received mercy, but
now you have received God's mercy.
1 Peter 2:10

Man walks a slim line clearly symbolized by the life of Paul – on one side of the line was his utter failure. On the other side of the line was the only thing deeper than his failure – the grace of Christ.

GOD REMEMBERS

So do not lose the courage you had in the past, which has a great reward. You must hold on, so you can do what God wants and receive what he has promised.
Hebrews 10:35-36

Do you ever wonder if everything will turn out right as long as you do everything right? Do you ever try to do something right and yet nothing seems to turn out like you planned? Take heart — when people do what is right, God remembers.

USE TIME WISELY

"Plant goodness, harvest the fruit of loyalty, plow the new ground of knowledge. Look for the Lord until he comes and pours goodness on you like water."
Hosea 10:12

Father, help us to use our time wisely, to take advantage of the opportunities we have to be just the type of Christians you want us to be. When it seems like we don't have enough time to do what we need to do, increase our gratitude for the challenges of each day. And help us meet those challenges in ways that please you.

ALLOW GOD TO HELP

So those who suffer as God wants should
trust their souls to the faithful Creator
as they continue to do what is right.
1 Peter 4:19

Something happens to us when we struggle with physical or emotional or financial problems. Either we can become paralyzed by our problems, turning inward and getting hooked on the "angel dust" of pity, or we can defeat the inclination to turn inward, and allow God to help us grow through these difficulties.

Grace Is A Free Gift

*All have sinned and are not good
enough for God's glory, and all
need to be made right with God
by his grace, which is a free gift.*
Romans 3:23-24

What is grace? It's what someone gives us
out of the goodness of their heart, not out
of the perfection of ours. The story of grace
is the good news that says that when we
come, he gives. That's what grace is.

MOTHERHOOD

*She watches over her family
and never wastes her time. Her
children speak well of her.*
Proverbs 31:27-28

There's something inherent about the qualities of motherhood that would cause anyone who questioned the existence of God to be convinced. What is it about motherhood that gives women six sets of hands, three pairs of eyes, a body with 180 parts, all replaceable, and the capacity to get by on coffee and leftovers?

SERVING OUT OF LOVE

Your rules are wonderful. That is why I keep them. Learning your words gives wisdom and understanding for the foolish.
Psalm 119:129-130

When you light somebody afire with the grace of God, you have a hard time putting him out. When you light people with legalism or with rules and regulations, they're going to burn out because they'll always live in fear. But a person set afire with the love of Jesus Christ will live in gratitude — serving his Lord out of love and not out of fear.

Valuable Qualities

But the Spirit produces the fruit of love, joy, peace, patience, kindness, goodness, faithfulness, gentleness, self-control.
Galatians 5:22-23

There are no perfect mothers. There are no perfect people. But someone in Scripture who teaches some valuable qualities we need as servants of God is Mary. She reminds us that God uses those who are willing, thoughtful, loyal, and faithful.

GOD'S POWER

*God's power protects you through
your faith until salvation is shown
to you at the end of time.*
1 Peter 1:5

The power of a strong relationship sustains us and gives us strength – it's that power in knowing, *If I fail, my friend is still there*, or, *If I fail, I have a wife who still loves me*. It's the power in knowing that – no matter what – we have a Father who still loves us.

BLESS THE MOTHERS

*Happy are those who respect the
Lord and obey him. You will
enjoy what you work for, and you
will be blessed with good things.*
Psalm 128:1-2

Father, bless the mothers of our world. As we think of the hands that guided us and those who are now guiding young lives, we stand before you on their behalf, in gratefulness and anticipation. And, Father, we pray a special prayer for those who yearn to be mothers but have yet to be graced with that child, asking for your special care and blessing on them.

STRENGTHEN YOURSELVES

*Since Christ suffered while he was
in his body, strengthen yourselves
with the same way of thinking
Christ had. The person who has
suffered in the body is finished with sin.*
1 Peter 4:1

As Jesus looked down from the cross, who did he see? He saw a loyal mother. To us, this was a moment of glory, but to Mary, it was the moment of her greatest pain. She was there, at that very last moment, to give that final word of strength, to weep that final maternal tear as her child made that final sacrifice.

GREAT THINGS

*The Lord has done great things
for us, and we are very glad.*
Psalm 126:3

What have we ever done to deserve the healing touch of Jesus to our souls? Nothing! Yet often we come to Jesus feeling pretty good about ourselves, saying, "Hey, I'll make a great contribution to your team." Hogwash! Jesus doesn't need us on his team. And he doesn't forgive us on the basis of what we've done. He forgives us on the basis of who he is.

MADE RIGHT

Being made right with God by his grace, we could have the hope of receiving the life that never ends.
Titus 3:7

Do you wonder where you can go for encouragement and motivation? Go back to that moment when you first saw the love of Jesus Christ. Remember the day when you were separated from Christ? You knew only guilt and confusion and then – a light. Someone opened a door and light came into your darkness, and you said in your heart, "I am redeemed!"

SPECIAL PONDERING

Now, my children, listen to me, because those who follow my ways are happy.
Proverbs 8:32

Praying for our children is a noble task. If what we are doing, in this fast-paced society, is taking us away from prayer time for our children, we're doing too much. There is nothing more special, more precious than that time that a parent spends struggling and pondering with God on behalf of a child.

NOT GUILTY!

Through Christ Jesus the law of the Spirit that brings life made me free from the law that brings sin and death.
Romans 8:2

Does the Word of God say, "There is *limited* condemnation for those who are in Christ Jesus"? No. Does it say, "There is *some* condemnation ... "? No. It says, "There is *no* condemnation for those who are in Christ Jesus." Think of it – regardless of our sin, we are not guilty!

LIBERATING GRACE

*God's grace has made me what I am
and his grace to me was not wasted.*
1 Corinthians 15:10

You know what happens when someone sees the grace of God? When someone really tastes the forgiving and liberating grace of God? Someone who tastes God's grace is the hardest worker, the most morally pure individual, and the person most willing to forgive.

THE TENDER-HEARTED JESUS

When Jesus saw Mary crying and the
Jews who came with her also crying,
he was upset and was deeply troubled.
John 11:33

Most of the people in the world have never seen the Jesus of the New Testament – a Redeemer whose eyes would swell with tears and whose heart would beat with passion. Most people serve a Redeemer only when they need a favor – a sort of magic Lord who's ignored except in time of crisis. We can't imitate a magic Jesus. The tender-hearted Jesus of the New Testament demands imitation by those who follow him.

Interested In Our Pain

*"This man was born blind so that
God's power could be shown in him."*
John 9:3

Jesus and his disciples saw a blind man
while walking down the road. The disciples said, "Jesus, who sinned?" Jesus said,
"No one sinned." Then Jesus healed the
man. And he eternally answered that our
pain is not a result of our sin. God is not so
small that he would zap us for making a
mistake. This passage teaches just the op-
posite: Our Savior is not asleep; Jesus is
alive and interested in our pain.

GUIDE US

"But be faithful, even if you have to die,
and I will give you the crown of life."
Revelation 2:10

Oh Father, for the surety that there is a truth in this world, we're thankful. For the assurance that there is a right and a wrong and you have always done what is right, we're thankful. We've all failed you; we've all taken wrong paths and made wrong choices. Guide us, Father. Enrich our conscience so that we may be faithful to the great and wonderful gift you've given us.

Waiting To Embrace Us

As the mountains surround Jerusalem, the Lord surrounds his people now and forever.
Psalm 125:2

We have a Father who is filled with compassion, a feeling Father who hurts when his children hurt. We serve a God who says that even when we're under pressure and feel like nothing is going to go right, he's waiting for us, to embrace us whether we succeed or fail.

ALL EQUALLY VALUABLE

*I wait for the Lord to help
me, and I trust his word.*
Psalm 130:5

When Jesus told the story of the missing
sheep, some of the people who were listen-
ing wiped away a tear because they knew
how it feels to be lost among the crowd.
Jesus wanted us to understand that we
have a Father who sees and cares for each
one of his children – that we are all equally
valuable to him.

JUNE

A PARENT'S PLEAS

Can't the creator of ears hear?
Can't the maker of eyes see?
Psalm 94:9

Never underestimate the ponderings of a Christian parent. Never underestimate the power that comes when a parent pleads with God on behalf of a child. Who knows how many prayers are being answered right now because of the faithful ponderings of a parent ten or twenty years ago? God listens to thoughtful parents.

JUNE 2

DOING WHAT'S RIGHT

Lord, let me live so people will praise you.
Psalm 143:11

Do what is right this week, whatever it is, whatever comes down the path, whatever problems and dilemmas you face – just do what's right. Maybe no one else is doing what's right, but you do what's right. You be honest. You take a stand. You be true. After all, regardless of what you do, God does what is right: he saves you with his grace.

JUNE 3

No Sin Too Deep

Keep yourselves in God's love as you wait for the Lord Jesus Christ with his mercy to give you life forever.
Jude verse 21

Father, we want to come home to you. But sometimes we're afraid that we've done something unforgivable, afraid that we've made you angry. And we wonder how you can forgive us. But Father, your Word teaches us that you will forgive us and that there's no sin too deep for your hand of forgiveness to reach.

JUNE 4

JOY WITH TROUBLE

We also have joy with our troubles, because we know that these troubles produce patience.
Romans 5:3

Sometimes people question God – "Is pain my punishment?" You've heard the expression "The rain falls on the just and the unjust" – or better, the unjust and the unjust, for we are all sinners. All of us are or will be victims of pain – it's simply a fact of our existence, regardless of how good or how bad we are. Life isn't fair? No, but there is one who justifies life and understands that pain.

THAT BRIDGE OF FRIENDSHIP

*Love means living the way God
commanded us to live. As you have
heard from the beginning, his
command is this: Live a life of love.*
2 John 1:6

We're in a fast-moving, fast-paced society. We need to build bridges between our hearts and those of people we see who need a friend – and allow Jesus to cross that bridge of friendship and walk into their hearts.

His Healing Hand

*The Lord helps those who have
been defeated and takes care
of those who are in trouble.*
Psalm 145:14

When Jesus healed the woman in Matthew 9, he told her that her faith had made her well. He was also saying to her, "You're very special to me, daughter. I know you don't have anything to offer me; I know you've been rejected by society, but your Father has not forgotten you." Our Savior says the same to us when we need his healing hand.

DEFEAT EVIL

Do not let evil defeat you,
but defeat evil by doing good.
Romans 12:21

Father, when we confront temptation, when we stand face to face with evil, we pray that you would give us strength and that you would use your power to block the path of evil.

JUNE 8

A Clear Conscience

*Keep a clear conscience so that those
who speak evil of your good life
in Christ will be made ashamed.*
1 Peter 3:16

Unresolved guilt is fatal. Unresolved
mistakes kill. And they don't just kill you,
they kill others. Unresolved errors cause us
to do what is illogical, cause us to explode
at someone who is innocent, cause someone
who has not participated in the sin to
receive the consequences.

RIGHT HERE!

My friends, do not be surprised at the terrible trouble which now comes to test you. Do not think that something strange is happening to you. But be happy that you are sharing in Christ's sufferings so that you will be happy and full of joy when Christ comes again in glory.
1 Peter 4:12-13

Where is God when we hurt? Where is he when sleep won't come? Where is he when we awaken in a hospital bed with pain that won't subside? He's right here! He hung on the gallows to prove once and for all that he's here — that he didn't create the hurt, but he came to take it away.

Your Enemy — The Evil One

The devil, your enemy, goes around like a roaring lion looking for someone to eat.
1 Peter 5:8

We should recognize who Satan is and not be afraid to point a finger at him. He is our enemy, and if we understand who the enemy is, we can better arm ourselves against him. The enemy in your marriage is not your spouse. The enemy at your work is not your employer or your employee. The enemy is not the system and not the church. The enemy is the evil one.

JUNE 11

LEARNING HOW TO TRUST GOD

I was put to death on the cross with Christ, and I do not live anymore – it is Christ who lives in me. I still live in my body, but I live by faith in the Son of God who loved me and gave himself to save me.
Galatians 2:20

It seems to me that learning how to trust God defines the meaning of Christian living. God doesn't wait until we have our moral life in order before he starts loving us. This is the inexpressible love of God.

JUNE 12

THE FAITHFUL WITNESS

Jesus is the faithful witness, the first among those raised from the dead. He is the ruler of the kings of the earth. He is the One who loves us, who made us free from our sins with the blood of his death.
Revelation 1:5

I want you to know something. When you hurt, God hurts with you. When no one listens to you, God listens to you. When you wipe away tears of loneliness or frustration or anguish, in heaven there's a pierced hand approaching a heavenly face wiping away a tear.

A Spirit Of Power

*God did not give us a spirit that
makes us afraid but a spirit of
power and love and self-control.*
2 Timothy 1:7

God can take that which no one else
would use and empower it like no one else
can.

A Different Kind
Of Freedom

*Live as free people, but do not
use your freedom as an excuse to do
evil. Live as servants of God.*
1 Peter 2:16

Freedom is an elusive thing – it's the carrot on the end of the stick that causes a lot of us mules to do the things we do. Jesus spoke of freedom, but he spoke of a different kind of freedom: the type of freedom that comes not through power but through submission. Not through control but through surrender. Not through possessions but through open hands.

To Be Faithful

"I am the One who searches hearts and minds, and I will repay each of you for what you have done."
Revelation 2:23

The task of fatherhood is to be faithful to the heavenly Father, to the spouse that God has given him, and to his children. If a father goes to his grave a pauper but is faithful on those three levels, he is a successful man.

JUNE 16

WHAT SWEETER BLESSING

Finally, all of you should be in agreement, understanding each other, loving each other as family, being kind and humble.
1 Peter 3:8

God blessed the commandment to honor our father and mother. He blessed it with a promise – a promise of joy, a promise of faithfulness. For what sweeter blessing is there than a family whose members shower honor on one another!

Prepare Your Heart

Look, Jesus is coming with the clouds and everyone will see him.
Revelation 1:7

Folks, if you're expecting to be given a fair shake in your life, forget it! You won't be. You're going to face illness. And your body is going to wear out. You may be the victim of someone else's mistake. But you can get through those tough times if you prepare your heart now, living to know and serve the Savior who loves you and died so that you might have an eternal home free of pain and sorrow.

JUNE 18

FAITHFUL LOVE

*"I want faithful love more than I want
animal sacrifices. I want people to know
me more than I want burnt offerings."*
Hosea 6:6

God loves those who need him most, who
rely on him, depend on him, and trust him
in everything. Little he cares whether
you've been as pure as John or as sinful as
Mary Magdalene; all that matters is your
trust in him.

BOLDNESS IN GOD'S PRESENCE

And this is the boldness we have in
God's presence: that if we ask God
for anything that agrees with what
he wants, he hears us. If we know he
hears us every time we ask him, we
know we have what we ask from him.
1 John 5:14-15

Father, help us today to maintain our promise of faithfulness to you, even in times
when we're not surrounded by people who
agree with us and encourage and understand our devotion to you. Give us great
courage as we face the challenges of each
new day.

COMFORTING OTHERS

*He comforts us every time we
have trouble, so when others have
trouble, we can comfort them with
the same comfort God gives us.*
2 Corinthians 1:4

Struggling with life's difficulties makes us
a little wiser, a little more capable, enabling
us to comfort others who experience pain.

A GESTURE OF AFFECTION

Do everything in love.
1 Corinthians 16:14

Never underestimate a gesture of affection. What you consider as wasted gestures may be the very thing that your child will never forget. If your child remembers anything, let him remember the tender affection that you had for him as a child.

A Certain Humility

*Pride will ruin people, but those
who are humble will be honored.*
Proverbs 29:23

I am frightened by our ability in America to convince ourselves that we don't need Jesus. We can amass fortunes, we can get degrees, we can own our house all on our own. And yet, there's a certain affluence that we can attain when we become poverty-stricken — a certain humility that comes with trials, that brings us face to face with the Savior.

The Kingdom Of Heaven

He made us to be a kingdom of
priests who serve God his Father.
To Jesus Christ be glory and
power forever and ever! Amen.
Revelation 1:6

The gospel is an easily understandable and transmittable message. The whole gospel can be brought down to one phrase: The kingdom of heaven is near! There's a King and there's a kingdom, and you can be a part of it. The choice is yours.

GOD'S LOVE FOR YOU

"Holy, holy, holy is the Lord God Almighty.
He was, he is, and he is coming."
Revelation 4:8

God's love for you is not dependent on how you look, how you think, how you act, or how perfect you are. His love is absolutely non-negotiable and non-returnable. Ours is a faithful God.

Set Your Priorities

So prepare your minds for service and have self-control. All your hope should be for the gift of grace that will be yours when Jesus Christ is shown to you.
1 Peter 1:13

Sometimes life gets confusing, doesn't it? Do you wake up with a list of things to do that is far longer than the hours you have? To set your priorities, find an answer to this question: Where do you want to be 100 years from now? If your answer is heaven, then your daily choices will have only one criteria: getting there!

GENUINE REPENTANCE

*"If my people, who are called by my name,
are sorry for what they have done, if they
pray and obey me and stop their evil ways,
I will hear them from heaven. I will forgive
their sin, and I will heal their land."*
2 Chronicles 7:14

Genuine repentance is a moving condition of the heart that is testified and demonstrated by our deeds. It's an inward conviction that expresses itself in outward actions.

DEMONSTRATE YOUR DEVOTION

Do what you learned and received from me, what I told you, and what you saw me do. And the God who gives peace will be with you.
Philippians 4:9

Oftentimes we say one thing and we do another. Paul, the apostle, says that all Christians are letters from Christ. People look at how you act before they look at what you say. We must demonstrate our devotion to Christ.

Embrace Us, Father

If I rise with the sun in the east and settle in the west beyond the sea, even there you would guide me. With your right hand you would hold me.
Psalm 139:9-10

God of heaven, we see your hand stretching as far as the east is from the west. Put your hands and your arms around us and embrace us, Father. Take us home. May we be yours forever.

HE IS THE WAY

But if anyone does sin, we have a helper in the presence of the Father – Jesus Christ, the One who does what is right. He is the way our sins are taken away, and not only our sins but the sins of all people.
1 John 2:1-2

What makes a Christian a Christian is not perfection but forgiveness.

FAN THE FLAME

"Here I am! I stand at the door and knock. If you hear my voice and open the door, I will come in and eat with you, and you will eat with me."
Revelation 3:20

Can you recall the moment you first believed? You felt a flame in your heart that was dancing so hot that you knew even death couldn't put it out. Is that flame still there? If it is, then fan it, bring it to life. Stand face to face with the only hope this earth knows.

JULY

JULY 1

IT'S NOT TOO LATE

*Lord, even when I have trouble all
around me, you will keep me alive. When
my enemies are angry, you will reach
down and save me by your power.*
Psalm 138:7

Regardless of what you've done, it's not
too late. Regardless of how far you've fallen,
it's not too late. It doesn't matter how low
the mistake is, it's not too late to dig down,
pull out that mistake, and let it go – and
be free.

"I'll Give You Eternity"

> *"God did not send his Son into the world to judge the world guilty, but to save the world through him."*
> John 3:17

Even if you've fallen, even if you've failed, even if everyone else has rejected you, Christ will not turn away from you. He came first and foremost to those who have no hope. He goes to those no one else would go to and says, "I'll give you eternity."

JULY 3

DON'T BE TOO PROUD

Don't be too proud in the Lord's presence, and he will make you great.
James 4:10

Indifference stirs the wrath of God: indifferent people who have grown spiritually dull, who are unresponsive, who see their own sinfulness and yet never fall to their knees and say, "I'm sorry, God."

JULY 4
RELEASED FROM
THAT BONDAGE

He will bring about what is right for me.
Then he will bring me out into the light,
and I will see him set things right.
Micah 7:9

We enjoy many freedoms in the United States. But unless you've been freed by God Almighty, there is one bondage you still carry, regardless of the country you're in. And that's the freedom of yesterday's regrets, yesterday's failures. All of us need to have that capacity and strength to stand tall with confidence that God has released us from that bondage of regret.

JULY 5
REALIZE THE URGENCY

*"So be eager to do right, and
change your hearts and lives."*
Revelation 3:19

What's the difference between a Christian
who's reaching out to people, trying to help
people — and a Christian who sits like a
fat cat on a pew? Well, maybe the Christian
who's reaching out realizes the urgency and
remembers what it was like before he knew
about Jesus. Maybe he realizes that when
people need help, they need Jesus above
all else.

A Sincere Regret

On the day I called to you, you answered me. You made me strong and brave.
Psalm 138:3

No one is happier than the one who has sincerely repented of wrong. Repentance is the decision to turn from selfish desires and seek God. It is a genuine, sincere regret that creates sorrow and moves us to admit wrong and desire to do better.

We Take Hope

His glory covers the skies, and his praise fills the earth. He is like a bright light. Rays of light shine from his hand, and there he hides his power.
Habakkuk 3:3-4

Father, you never promised us that this world would be easy. And yet, all of us can look ahead to the city that's set on a hill, to the lights that call us to eternity. And we take hope.

JULY 8

LORD, I WILL THANK YOU

*Lord, I will thank you with
all my heart; I will sing to you.*
Psalm 138:1

It's incredible that anyone could look at the kindness of God, the faithfulness of God, and the goodness of God and not feel any emotion of gratitude.

LISTEN AS GOD TEACHES

The Lord corrects those he loves, just as parents correct the child they delight in.
Proverbs 3:12

The struggles that you're going through now – don't discard them. Listen to God as he teaches you so that you can teach others. You see, a time of suffering teaches us something we never knew before and may prepare us for a time of counsel that we will give someone years from now.

LIFE'S BATTLEGROUND

*Our fight is not against people on
earth but against the rulers and
authorities and the powers of this
world's darkness, against the spiritual
powers of evil in the heavenly world.*
Ephesians 6:12

Where's our battleground in life? Is our
battle against our neighbor? Is our battle
against our family? No. The battle is with
the invisible forces of evil, the black one
that has invaded the earth, whose goal is
to win the battle within every Christian.
Satan failed in his desire to control God,
and it's only with God's help that we can
defeat him.

JULY 11

CLARIFY WHAT YOUR TASK IS

*Always be ready to answer
everyone who asks you to explain
about the hope you have.*
1 Peter 3:15

Do you want to simplify your life? Then clarify what your task is. What are the words, what are the concepts, what message do you want to transmit to your friends and family? The truth of Jesus Christ is the simple truth of his sacrifice.

THE LORD IS GOOD

*The Lord is good, giving
protection in times of trouble.
He knows who trusts in him.*
Nahum 1:7

A lot of us live with a hidden fear that God is angry at us. Somewhere, sometime, some Sunday school class or some television show convinced us that God has a whip behind his back, a paddle in his back pocket, and he's going to nail us when we've gone too far. No concept could be more wrong! Your Savior's Father is very fond of you and only wants to share his love with you.

THE ROAD TO EVERLASTING LIFE

See if there is any bad thing in me.
Lead me on the road to everlasting life.
Psalm 139:24

Father in heaven, help us as we cope and grapple with yesterday's failures. They dog at our heels like irritations. They follow us around. They cling to our ankles like fifteen-pound ball weights. Help us to release those regrets in the right way, and keep us close.

THE VOICE OF GOD

God, your thoughts are precious to me.
They are so many! If I could count them,
they would be more than all the grains of
sand. When I wake up, I am still with you.
Psalm 139:17-18

Recreation rebuilds the interior of man.
It's not just getting out and playing golf;
it's being so silent that you can hear the
voice of God.

THE FIRE THAT CAN'T BE PUT OUT

The Lord will be King forever. Jerusalem, your God is everlasting. Praise the Lord!
Psalm 146:10

Those who have been redeemed just can't keep quiet. There's something about the fire that burns in their hearts that even the winds of secularism and humanism and peer pressure just can't put it out.

BORN AGAIN

You have been born again, and this new life did not come from something that dies, but from something that cannot die. You were born again through God's living message that continues forever.
1 Peter 1:23

When a Christian becomes a follower of Christ, he dies to himself. And the life that he possesses is the life to come, not this life on earth.

GOOD REIGNS SUPREME

*God, you have heard my
promises. You have given me what
belongs to those who fear you.*
Psalm 61:5

Father, thank you for your promise that if
we do what is right, eventually truth and
justice and goodness will prevail. As we
face the dilemmas and options of this time,
remind us that good does reign supreme.

TREASURES IN HEAVEN

Store your treasures in heaven
where they cannot be destroyed
by moths or rust and where thieves
cannot break in and steal them.
Matthew 6:20

The kingdom never advances because of our possessions. It advances because of our faith. "Lean on me," says Jesus. He needs us to depend on him rather than on our possessions.

TOSS IT AWAY

"Though your sins are like scarlet, they can be white as snow. Though your sins are deep red, they can be white like wool."
Isaiah 1:18

Sometimes we try to deal with a mistake by covering it up with more mistakes, or by repressing it, or by justifying it. That's like walking around with a pebble in our shoe – it causes us so much frustration that our whole body compensates for its presence, when all we have to do is take it out and toss it away.

Give, And You Will Receive

*"Give, and you will receive. You will
be given much. Pressed down, shaken
together, and running over, it will spill
into your lap. The way you give to others
is the way God will give to you."*
Luke 6:38

God doesn't want us because of what we
have to offer him; he wants us because *he*
has everything to offer *us*. God doesn't
want you because you have certain gifts to
offer. He wants to give you gifts so that
you then can offer them to other people.

THE PURITY OF YOUR FAITH

The purity of your faith will bring
you praise and glory and honor
when Jesus Christ is shown to you.
1 Peter 1:7

Father, we believe that when we see you, any suffering that we endured on the face of this earth will be worth it. We believe that the first five minutes we stand in heaven we will know that anything we endured on this globe will be forgotten. Father, help us to understand. And when we cannot understand, help us to trust.

TELL THE GOOD NEWS

*"Go everywhere in the world, and
tell the Good News to everyone."*
Mark 16:15

The most important thing we can do on this earth is reach out and help those who have not yet found the key to that life that is to come.

God Calls Us To Pray

*The Lord is close to everyone who prays
to him, to all who truly pray to him.*
Psalm 145:18

When God says to pray, he really means
it. To pray is the most commonly men-
tioned command in Scripture. It is men-
tioned more than "love your neighbor,"
more than "go to church," and more than
"evangelize." More than anything else, God
calls us to pray.

ALL OF THAT AND MORE!

"Amen! Praise, glory, wisdom, thanks,
honor, power, and strength belong to
our God forever and ever. Amen!"
Revelation 7:12

Father, had you not become flesh and dwelt among us, had you not treated us with mercy and kindness, had you not loved us beyond our worth, you'd still be God. You'd still be worthy of our praise. And you'd still be holy. Yet, Father, you did all of that and more.

TIMELESS TRUTHS

Don't make me either rich or poor; just give me enough food for each day. If I have too much, I might reject you and say, "I don't know the Lord." If I am poor, I might steal and disgrace the name of my God.
Proverbs 30:8-9

Father, help us to see what is important, what is eternal, and what is lasting. Let us make decisions based on our eternal life and not on temporary possessions. Father, help us to put into practice the timeless truths found in your Word. And most of all, Father, thank you for loving us.

FORGIVE EACH OTHER

Get along with each other,
and forgive each other. If someone
does wrong to you, forgive that
person because the Lord forgave you.
Colossians 3:13

Jesus says, "Use your head, but don't lower your standards." You be the one who interrupts that vicious cycle of paying one another back. Don't get on the roller coaster of resentment and anger. You be the one who says, "Yes, he mistreated me, but I am going to be like Christ. I'll be the one who says, 'Forgive them, Father, they don't know what they're doing.'"

STAND STRONG IN THE LORD

*My dear brothers and sisters, I love you
and want to see you. You bring me joy
and make me proud of you, so stand
strong in the Lord as I have told you.*
Philippians 4:1

A Christian in his surroundings should
encourage everyone to be better, instead of
being the one who stoops to be like everyone else.

HOPE IS THE ANCHOR
FOR YOUR SOUL

*Through Christ you believe
in God, who raised Christ from
the dead and gave him glory. So
your faith and your hope are in God.*
1 Peter 1:21

Our hope is the anchor for the soul. "Where's your hope?" Jesus asks. It is the confident hope of the return of Christ.

"Do Not Worry"

*I have taken your words to heart
so I would not sin against you.*
Psalm 119:11

The same God that gave us commandments such as "Do not commit adultery, do not murder" said, "Do not worry." It's a violation of our relationship to God to question his authority by worrying.

LORD, HEAR MY PRAYER

*Lord, hear my prayer, and listen when
I ask for mercy. I call to you in times
of trouble, because you will answer me.*
Psalm 86:6-7

Nobody else on the face of the earth is praying to God except Christians. That's why Christians must be about the business of intercessory prayer. When we encounter battles and struggles in life, the first step of the Christian is to pray. Every time we pray about something, every time we sincerely take something to God, God handles it, and God deals with it.

WITH THE HOPE PROMISED US

If you are beaten for doing wrong, there is no reason to praise you for being patient in your punishment. But if you suffer for doing good, and you are patient, then God is pleased.
1 Peter 2:20

Sometimes it seems when we try to do something good, the more bad things happen, doesn't it? It's tough to have problems when you are trying to be a faithful servant of God, or trying to be loyal to your family. Life was not designed to be problem free, but with the hope promised us by the Father, we can handle the problems that come into our daily life.

AUGUST

PURE LIKE CHRIST

Christ is pure, and all who have this hope in Christ keep themselves pure like Christ.
1 John 3:3

God says you're on your way to becoming a disciple when you can keep a clear head and a pure heart.

GRACIOUS TO US

"You are worthy, our Lord and God, to receive glory and honor and power, because you made all things. Everything existed and was made, because you wanted it."
Revelation 4:11

Father in heaven, hear our praise. Holy Father, we are thankful that we have more than enough clothes to wear, thankful that we have places to sleep and that we won't go to bed hungry. We're thankful that even if all of this were taken away from us, we'd still have our hope of eternity. You have been gracious to us.

THE LORD GOD IS MY STRENGTH

The Lord God is my strength. He makes me like a deer that does not stumble so I can walk on the steep mountains.
Habakkuk 3:19

As long as we have hope, as long as we recognize that this world is not our home, as long as we recognize that some day all of our problems will be solved, that is where we will gather our strength.

AUGUST 4

WALK THROUGH THAT DOOR

*"You will not succeed by your
own strength or power, but by my
Spirit," says the Lord All-Powerful.*
Zechariah 4:6

God has opened a door for you. Now you
can choose to spend the rest of your life
enslaved by guilt and remorse, or you can
walk through that door and close it behind you.

GOD KNOWS YOUR NAME

I will bow down facing your holy Temple, and I will thank you for your love and loyalty. You have made your name and your word greater than anything.
Psalm 138:2

Doesn't it feel good when people remember your name? I really appreciate it when people remember my name. I used to wonder why God would have all those lists of people's names in the Bible. The answer is that those names are important to God – he knows all those names, just as he knows yours and mine.

AUGUST 6

WRITTEN IN YOUR BOOK

All the days planned for me were written in your book before I was one day old.
Psalm 139:16

You know, we really don't know what to pray for, do we? What if God had answered every prayer that you ever prayed? Just think who you'd be married to. Just think where you'd be living. Just think what you'd be doing.

FORGIVE OUR DOUBTS

Lord, you do everything for me.
Lord, your love continues forever.
Psalm 138:8

Father, forgive us for the times that we have questioned you; forgive us for the times we have doubted you; forgive us for the times we've shaken our heads and pounded our fists against the earth and cried, "Where are you?" For Father, we know that you have been here – you've carried us through the valley and you've given us strength.

GRAB THAT ANCHOR
OF THE SOUL

*You are receiving the goal of your
faith – the salvation of your souls.*
1 Peter 1:9

One thing no one can take away from you
is your faith. This world can and may take
everything you have. But no one can take
away your faith. Grab that faith; clutch
tightly that anchor of the soul.

God Forgives All Our Mistakes

*God, examine me and know my heart;
test me and know my nervous thoughts.*
Psalm 139:23

Revealing our feelings is the beginning of healing. Articulating what's on our heart, confessing our mistakes, is the first step in seeing that God can forgive those mistakes and all others.

Our Guide Through Life

"The Lord your God is with you; the mighty One will save you. He will rejoice over you. You will rest in his love; he will sing and be joyful about you."
Zephaniah 3:17

Father, we invite you to be our guide through life. Lord, we don't ask that you take from us the worries of this life but that you surface the worries of this life so that we can share them with you and turn them over to you.

AN ANCHOR IN
THE LAND TO COME

"At that time I will gather you; at that time I will bring you back home. I will give you honor and praise from people everywhere when I make things go well again for you, as you will see with your own eyes."
Zephaniah 3:20

Within each of us is a desire to know what lies ahead, a desire to have hope, a desire to have an anchor cast in the land to come so that we can endure the land of today.

AUGUST 12

RECOGNIZE THE GIVER

"Fear God and give him praise, because the time has come for God to judge all people. So worship God who made the heavens, and the earth, and the sea, and the springs of water."
Revelation 14:7

Isn't it ironic that times of trouble remind us that we live by God's blessings and not by our own goodness? We grow accustomed to our blessings so much that when our blessings aren't there, we begin to truly recognize them and the Giver as well.

WE GIVE YOU PRAISE

Yes, God made all things, and everything continues through him and for him. To him be the glory forever! Amen.
Romans 11:36

Dear Father, we give you praise. We honor and glorify your name. You truly are the King of kings and the Lord of lords. We thank you and worship you and glorify your name forever and ever.

PUT YOUR ANXIETIES ON HIM

*Give all your worries to him,
because he cares about you.*
1 Peter 5:7

God wants you to put your anxieties on him. Let him do your worrying for you because he is faithful. When you read this verse, substitute your own name for the word *you*. Isn't that good to hear?

No More Pain

*"He will wipe away every tear from their eyes,
and there will be no more death, sadness, crying
or pain, because all the old ways are gone."*
Revelation 21:4

Father, you never said there would be a day with no rain. You never said there would be life with no pain. But you did promise that if we would endure, we would be saved.

AUGUST 16

GOD'S PURPOSE

*"I will make my people strong, and
they will live as I say," says the Lord.*
Zechariah 10:12

There is an eternal purpose. There is a great
river of God's purpose that is moving
toward an eternal home with him. You
can't stop God's purpose. God's purpose
is greater than you are, and if you are God's
child, nothing is going to slow down God's
purpose for your life.

GIVE US GUIDANCE

Teach me to do what you want,
because you are my God. Let your
good Spirit lead me on level ground.
Psalm 143:10

Lord, help us search your Word for practical help in our daily lives. Help us to lean on you, and help us to turn to you first. Give us, O Father, your strength and guidance, and increase our hope.

Control My Tongue

*Lord, help me control my tongue;
help me be careful about what I say.
Take away my desire to do evil or
to join others in doing wrong.*
Psalm 141:3-4

When we avoid dealing with our mistakes
and pretend they don't exist, they usually
express themselves in ways that we would
not anticipate: anger at someone else,
frustration at something else, lack of
control.

SUCH LOVE!

The Lord is pleased with those who respect him, with those who trust his love.
Psalm 147:11

God loves us so much that sometimes he gives us what we need and not what we ask.

You Have Been Made Holy

"Everyone will respect you, Lord, and will honor you. Only you are holy. All the nations will come and worship you, because the right things you have done are now made known."
Revelation 15:4

We've been offered so much – when you realize that you have been made holy in God's eyes by the purification of his grace, doesn't it make you want to stay pure? Doesn't this realization make you want to keep from staining God's precious creature that is you?

A DOGGED FAITH

I will praise the Lord all my life; I will sing praises to my God as long as I live.
Psalm 146:2

Make your faith an independent dogged faith, firmly planted in God's sacrificed Son on the hill of Calvary. It can never be taken away from you.

AUGUST 22

GOD IS IN CONTROL

*"God's holy people must be patient.
They must obey God's commands
and keep their faith in Jesus."*
Revelation 14:12

Sometimes storms of life come to teach us
that God is in control, that we must lean
on him and learn to be thankful for the
richness of his blessings to us.

God Is With You

Everything the Lord does is right.
He is loyal to all he has made.
Psalm 145:17

God is with you. God is with you! The same God that guided his Son through death and back to life said he will never leave us or forsake us. He is right there with you, perhaps even more in times of crisis than any other time.

AUGUST 24

HE PROTECTS ME

*Praise the Lord, my Rock, who trains
me for war, who trains me for battle.
He protects me like a strong, walled city,
and he loves me. He is my defender and
my Savior, my shield and my protection.*
Psalm 144:1-2

You may look ahead and see some crisis coming down the pike and think, *I'll never be able to handle that.* You probably couldn't right now, but God is with you, and he will give you the strength you need.

AUGUST 25

God Doesn't Lie

*"Hallelujah! Salvation, glory, and
power belong to our God, because
his judgments are true and right."*
Revelation 19:1-2

When God makes a promise, he doesn't
lie. And his promises are that everything
is going to reach fruition someday. Those
who have opted to follow God will be with
God forever, and everything else will make
sense.

AUGUST 26

A Purpose In Our Pain

*We share in the many sufferings of
Christ. In the same way, much
comfort comes to us through Christ.*
2 Corinthians 1:5

When we face struggles, we often wonder,
Why? Years from now, though, we may
realize that it was those struggles that
taught us something we could not have
otherwise learned – that there was a
purpose in our pain.

FORGET THE FAILURES
OF THE PAST

*"Everything that is hidden will be made clear
and every secret thing will be made known."*
Mark 4:22

I wonder if we stay so busy because we're trying to forget yesterday's failures. We do need to forget those failures of the past, but if we never stop to deal with them, the guilt over those old mistakes will hound us and nip at our heels like an ill-behaved puppy.

AUGUST 28

OPEN TO THE COUNSEL OF GOD

Good people will praise his name;
honest people will live in his presence.
Psalm 140:13

In this fast-paced world in which we live, the very thing we need to do is what we often don't do: We need simply to sit still and open our heart to the counsel of God. Then we will be well prepared for whatever the day brings.

AUGUST 29

Rejoice And Be Happy

*"Hallelujah! Our Lord God, the
Almighty, rules. Let us rejoice and
be happy and give God glory."*
Revelation 19:6-7

Father, as we set about the task of trying
to be your people, we pray that you'll help
us. May we glorify your name, may we be
open-minded, may we be sincere, may we
be willing to change and grow. We thank
you, Lord, for the privilege of being your
people.

A Greater Purpose

*When a person's steps follow the
Lord, God is pleased with his ways.
If he stumbles, he will not fall,
because the Lord holds his hand.*
Psalm 37:23-24

God's purpose is greater than your pain,
and he has a greater purpose than your
problems. Your crises are not going to slow
down the purpose of God – have confidence
in that.

FORGET THOSE HURTS!

He can help those who are tempted, because he himself suffered and was tempted.
Hebrews 2:18

Resentment is when you allow your hurts to turn to hates. When those hates simmer in your heart, they create bitterness and you are the one who suffers. Forget those hurts!

SEPTEMBER

A WORD OF HOPE

The Lord's love never ends; his mercies never stop. They are new every morning; Lord, your loyalty is great. I say to myself, "The Lord is mine, so I hope in him."
Lamentations 3:22-24

What do you need most today? Do you need just a word of hope? That's what we all need. And that's what the Word of God does that nothing and no one else can. The Word of God says to us that there is no hopeless situation, no hopeless illness, no hopeless marriage. If there were hopeless situations, then God would have given up long ago.

THE CONFIDENCE OF FORGIVENESS

Lord, you are kind and forgiving and have great love for those who call to you.
Psalm 86:5

It's never too late to get a second chance with God. It's never too late! Think about Paul – he had been a murderer and a blasphemer. He had to look into the faces of people whose fathers he had persecuted, whose children he had killed. He could have spent his life looking at yesterday, but he didn't do that. He started life over again in the confidence of his forgiveness.

THIS HOPE NEVER DISAPPOINTS

And patience produces character, and character produces hope. And this hope will never disappoint us, because God has poured out his love to fill our hearts.
Romans 5:4-5

Here's a checklist of criteria for handling problems: a clear head, a clean heart, a calm soul, and a confident hope.

THE PROMISE OF SALVATION

"Then the Lord will be king over the whole world: At that time there will be only one Lord, and his name will be the only name."
Zechariah 14:9

Father, you've given us such a great promise, the promise of salvation. Forgive us, Father, when we sometimes put more hope in the things of this earth than in the incredible promises of your heaven.

A VIRTUE THAT BRINGS MUCH JOY

Remember to welcome strangers, because some who have done this have welcomed angels without knowing it.
Hebrews 13:2

Here's a suggestion: We should all wear antennas to work, to church, to school — antennas that pick up on people who seem out of place, whose loneliness shows. Why not be the one to approach these folks and extend friendship to them? Maybe you think the last thing you need is another friend. But friendliness — hospitality — is a virtue that brings as much joy to the giver as to the receiver.

THE GREAT DEPTH OF YOUR LOVE

But God shows his great love for us in this way: Christ died for us while we were still sinners.
Romans 5:8

Holy Father, you did not have to save us. You didn't have to touch us. Who would have blamed you for turning your back on the mess that we've made out of this world and allowing us to spin off into oblivion? But when you saw our pain, you came. When you heard our cries, you hastened. Thank you, Father, for the great depth of your love that never ends.

THE CROSS IS STILL THERE

"Lord, all our success is because of what you have done, so give us peace."
Isaiah 26:12

In the midst of your busy-ness, the Cross is still there. In the midst of your empti-ness, the Cross is still there. The promises of Jesus still stand today. You can claim peace in the midst of a hectic life – not without sacrifice or concentration, but you can do it.

Part Of An Eternal Plan

*His purpose was that through the church
all the rulers and powers in the heavenly
world will now know God's wisdom.*
Ephesians 3:10

The concept of Christ's followers being called the church is part of an eternal purpose. It is something that was dreamed long before the mountains were dreamed up, long before the oceans were conceived, long before the stars were created. We are part of an eternal plan.

SEPTEMBER 9

BEGIN THE HEALING PROCESS

The God who gives peace be with you all.
Romans 15:33

Are you hurting today? Maybe you need to touch the hem of the Savior's garment. Maybe you need to come home to the only one who has the power to heal your hurting heart. I pray that this will be the day to begin the healing process.

THIS PRECIOUS COMMODITY

God ... will give you all the seed you need and make it grow so there will be a great harvest from your goodness. He will make you rich in every way so that you can always give freely. And your giving ... will cause many to give thanks to God.
2 Corinthians 9:10-11

Never before have parents been in such dire straits for this precious commodity we call time. Moms and dads drive an hour to get to work and an hour to get home. By the time they get home, they have to get ready and go to another meeting. There is no way we can be successful parents without giving our children that faithful element of time.

The Same Holy Spirit

We know that we live in God and he lives in us, because he gave us his Spirit ... Whoever confesses that Jesus is the Son of God has God living inside, and that person lives in God.
1 John 4:13, 15

The same Holy Spirit that operates wonderfully inside a person is the exact power that went into a dark tomb where lay the broken and lifeless body of Jesus Christ, and somehow, in a way that no human being can ever explain, breathed life-giving power into that body.

SEE JESUS IN A NEW WAY

*We must not become tired of doing good.
We will receive our harvest of eternal life
at the right time if we do not give up.*
Galatians 6:9

Lift up our eyes, Father, that we might
see our world as you see it. Hold up our
hearts, Father, that we might respond as
you respond to the hurts around us. Lord,
would you restore the spirit of undying
gratitude? May we each day see Jesus in a
fresh and new way?

Lay Your Cares At His Feet

*Wait for the Lord's help and
follow him. He will honor you
and give you the land, and you
will see the wicked sent away.*
Psalm 37:34

Only you can surrender your concerns to
the Father. No one else can take those away
and give them to God. Only you can cast
all your anxieties on the one who cares for
you. What better way to start the day than
laying your cares at his feet?

SEPTEMBER 14

CHILDREN OF GOD

*"But to all who did accept him
and believe in him he gave the
right to become children of God."*
John 1:12

Father, you are God and Creator, but we
come to you as children coming to their
father, as children who would ask their
father to hold and comfort them, hoping
to receive words of wisdom.

MAKE ME STRONG AGAIN

*I am sad and tired. Make me strong
again as you have promised.*
Psalm 119:28

Pain is inevitable, but misery is optional.

LISTEN TO YOUR OWN HEART

My God, I want to do what you want.
Your teachings are in my heart.
Psalm 40:8

The majority is not always right. If the majority had ruled, the children of Israel never would have left Egypt. They would have voted to stay in bondage. If the majority had ruled, David would have never fought Goliath. His brothers would have voted for him to stay with the sheep. What's the point? You must listen to your own heart.

KEEP US CLOSE TO YOU

Let everyone who trusts you be happy; let them sing glad songs forever. Protect those who love you and who are happy because of you.
Psalm 5:11

Heavenly Father, may your name be praised. Lord, may we see the joy that is before us? Would you pull back the eternal curtain and give us a glimpse into the everlasting? Would you hear the secret yearnings of our hearts? Will you keep us close to you this day?

THE COURAGE TO WONDER

They love the Lord's teachings,
and they think about those teachings
day and night. They are strong,
like a tree planted by a river.
Psalm 1:2-3

All of us, Father, at one time or another, have wondered if you really are who you say you are. We've looked at the consequences and circumstances of our life, and wondered why these things happen. We have the courage to wonder, when we read page after page in the Bible sharing the agony of those who sought you. And we find great encouragement from those who found you.

I Will Trust The Lord

If an army surrounds me,
I will not be afraid. If war
breaks out, I will trust the Lord.
Psalm 27:3

There has never been a time in the history of this globe when there was not a rain cloud somewhere on the earth. There may be blue skies for us occasionally, but the rain always comes. So, instead of looking for ways to escape problems, look for methods to face them head on.

THINKING GROUNDED IN THE WORD

I call to you, God, and you answer me.
Psalm 17:6

Anchor your convictions to the Word of God to help prevent crises from occurring in your life. When facing tough decisions, employ dogged and determined prayer and thinking grounded in the Word.

Help Us To See Jesus

*"I am the Alpha and the Omega, the
Beginning and the End. I will give
free water from the spring of the water
of life to anyone who is thirsty."*
Revelation 21:6

Father, we want to see you and know you
better. We ask you, Father, to help us see
Jesus and to deepen our faith upon seeing
him more clearly.

GET YOUR BRAIN IN GEAR

*"Listen, I am sending you out like
sheep among wolves. So be as smart
as snakes and as innocent as doves."*
Matthew 10:16

Don't retire your brain when you become
a follower of Christ. Be a thinker. Jesus told
his followers to be shrewd as snakes. The
first thing you need to do to solve problems
is to get your brain in gear! That may not
sound very spiritual, but it's a very practical principle. You need to use your head.

THE PROMISE OF ETERNAL LIFE

We all share in Christ if we keep till the end the sure faith we had in the beginning.
Hebrews 3:14

Father, teach us to set our hopes on heaven, to hold firmly to the promise of eternal life, so that we can withstand the struggles and storms of this world. May your holy Word be a soothing medicine to the wounded heart.

THE LORD PROTECTS MY LIFE

*The Lord is my light and the one
who saves me. I fear no one. The Lord
protects my life; I am afraid of no one.*
Psalm 27:1

The Christian in the midst of a crisis doesn't allow everyone's opinion or everyone's feelings to cause him to drift away from what is most important. He sets his anchor deep in the Word and firm in his faith.

HAVING A SAVIOR IN CHRIST

*I pray that the faith you share
may make you understand every
blessing we have in Christ.*
Philemon verse 6

Having a Savior in Christ means that the
hopeless have hope, the dead have life, and
the abandoned have Good News.

THE NATURE OF REPENTANCE

This is what the Lord God, the Holy One of Israel says: "If you come back to me and trust me, you will be saved. If you will be calm and trust me, you will be strong."
Isaiah 30:15

You look at the love of God and you can't believe he's loved you like he has, and it motivates you to change your life. That is the nature of repentance.

THE FRESH AIR OF GOD'S FORGIVENESS

"Hear their prayers from your home in heaven. Forgive and treat each person as he should be treated because you know what is in a person's heart. Only you know what is in people's hearts."
2 Chronicles 6:30

Could you use the genuine fresh air of God's forgiveness? Would you love to stand in the approval of God again? How do you do it? By genuinely admitting to God that you've made a mistake, knowing that God loves you more than he hates your mistakes. And knowing that he will forgive those mistakes.

ANOTHER KINGDOM

I will be glad and rejoice in your love, because you saw my suffering; you knew my troubles. You have not handed me over to my enemies but have set me in a safe place.
Psalm 31:7-8

Jesus went against the grain. The Messiah was expected to appear like a conquering king heading for the castle. Instead, he spoke of another kingdom. And he spent his time out in the countryside, preaching tenderness, meekness, love, and kindness rather than fire and punishment.

A Difference Between Faith And Presumption

The Lord shows his true love
every day. At night I have a song,
and I pray to my living God.
Psalm 42:8

I believe there's great power in prayer. I believe God heals the wounded, and that he can raise the dead. But I don't believe we tell God what to do and when to do it. You see, there's a difference between faith and presumption. There's a difference between believing he's the almighty God and demanding he become our divine servant.

ASK ANY QUESTION

But I will call to God for help,
and the Lord will save me. Morning,
noon, and night I am troubled and
upset, but he will listen to me.
Psalm 55:16-17

It's not a sin to doubt. Disbelief is sin, but questioning – sincerely seeking – is acceptable to God because in the presence of God you may ask any question you want.

OCTOBER

OCTOBER 1

THE TRUE TEST OF FAITH

*If we are not faithful, he
will still be faithful, because he
cannot be false to himself.*
2 Timothy 2:13

It's not hard to have faith when all of our bills are being paid and our kids are healthy and our marriage is intact. It's not hard to have faith when God gives us everything we want. The true test of faith comes when circumstances are difficult, when our train of hope gets derailed.

Proclaim God's Mercy

Your kingdom is built on what is right and fair. Love and truth are in all you do.
Psalm 89:14

What are Christians to proclaim? We are to proclaim God's mercy. First and foremost, we must announce to the world that God is a good God. We need to be a source of Good News. And we need to be a source of comfort.

OCTOBER 3

OUR GOAL

In every way be an example of doing good deeds. When you teach, do it with honesty and seriousness.
Titus 2:7

If we ever get to the point where our goal is to have people say, "What a wonderful person," we're missing the mark. Instead, our goal is to have people say, "What a wonderful God this person serves." Our task is to have people say, "Tell me about your God," to point people to him.

Messengers Of God's Grace

*God has chosen you and
made you his holy people.*
Colossians 3:12

We should be messengers of God's grace. We should be with the poor what Christ would be with the poor. We should be with the lost what Christ would be with the lost. We should be with the discouraged what Christ would be with the discouraged ... with the sick, the lonely, exactly what Christ would be.

YOU ARE THE LIGHT

*"You are the light that gives
light to the world. A city that is
built on a hill cannot be hidden."*
Matthew 5:14

When you extend hospitality to others, you're not trying to impress people, you're trying to reflect God to them. You don't have to be rich to be hospitable. A wise friend once told me, "If you won't give people hot dogs when you're poor, you won't give them steaks when you're rich." We shouldn't let our pride get in the way of being hospitable.

Do You Have Faith?

Faith means being sure of the things we hope for and knowing that something is real even if we do not see it.
Hebrews 11:1

Do you have faith? If you have faith, then you have what it takes to tackle your problems before they tackle you. If you have that confident hope, then you will know how to handle whatever life brings you.

OUR QUEST TO REST

"Come to me, all of you who are tired and have heavy loads, and I will give you rest."
Matthew 11:28

Perhaps the words of the carpenter, promising rest, are so compelling because of our endless desire and quest to rest – not just to rest in the body, but to rest the heart, to find peace, to finally settle down in a valley fertile with contentment.

OCTOBER 8

USE YOUR GOD-GIVEN GIFT

*There are different kinds of gifts,
but they are all from the same
Spirit. There are different ways
to serve but the same Lord to serve.*
1 Corinthians 12:4-5

You can develop a God-given gift. You may have the gift of encouragement or the gift of teaching or some other gift. What you do with that gift is up to you. You can use your God-given gift to let Christ shine through you.

Do Not Hold Back Your Mercy

Lord, do not hold back your mercy from me; let your love and truth always protect me.
Psalm 40:11

Father, you promised that there would be faith and strength and hope to meet life's problems. Father, give that strength to those whose anxieties have buried their dreams, whose illnessess have hospitalized their hopes, whose burdens are bigger than their shoulders.

YOKED WITH JESUS

"The path of life is level for those who are right with God; Lord, you make the way of life smooth for those people."
Isaiah 26:7

Jesus says, "Take my yoke." He had made countless yokes as a carpenter. (A yoke is that instrument that joins two oxen so they can work together.) But before we can be yoked with Jesus, we have to admit we need him, don't we? A lot of us are out there plowing on our own, dragging a yoke where Jesus is supposed to be.

THE FIRST STEP

Turn your face from my sins and wipe out all my guilt. Create in me a pure heart, God, and make my spirit right again.
Psalm 51:9-10

The first step toward pardon is the admission of guilt. The first step toward forgiveness is the request for forgiveness.

THE ONLY PATH TO CONTENTMENT

Do not love the world or the things in the world. If you love the world, the love of the Father is not in you.
1 John 2:15

Do you feel that you've spent your life in endless pursuit of contentment? Do you reach the top of the ladder, and discover you don't want to be there any more? Do you dream about having the perfect mate, and once you marry, you realize he or she isn't perfect? Contentment is not found in things of this world; the only path to contentment is through Christ.

JESUS – ANGRY?

*Then Jesus criticized the cities
where he did most of his miracles,
because the people did not change
their lives and stop sinning.*
Matthew 11:20

Jesus – angry? His fists clenched and his eyebrows furrowed, his face getting red, his veins bulging in his neck, and he's angry. He demands that the people repent.

SIMPLY TRUST THE LORD

I was very worried, but you comforted me and made me happy.
Psalm 94:19

Has any good ever come out of any worrying that you've ever done? Worry only compartmentalizes us and makes us unable to do what we set out to do. If you are worried about a problem, what you need to do is simply trust the Lord and do good.

HIS LAST PUBLIC INVITATION

*"Accept my teachings and learn from me,
because I am gentle and humble in spirit,
and you will find rest for your lives."*
Matthew 11:29

Jesus takes a deep breath and turns and looks into the weary faces of the farmers and housewives and businessmen who've come to hear him speak, and he offers what some consider to be his last public invitation.

OCTOBER 16

COMBAT IS OPTIONAL

*"Do to others what you would want
them to do to you ... Then you will
have a great reward, and you will be
children of the Most High God."*
Luke 6:31, 35

Conflict is inevitable, but combat is optional. Use your God-given creative energy to solve conflict before it escalates into combat.

Extend Your Forgiveness

Lord, if you punished people for all their sins, no one would be left, Lord. But you forgive us, so you are respected.
Psalm 130:3-4

Extend your forgiveness. If you have been forgiven by God, then there is room for you to forgive another human being. If God has forgiven you, then there is a wellspring of mercy from which you can draw and give to someone else. No one has offended you more than you have already offended God!

Repairing A Relationship

"You, Lord, give true peace to those who depend on you, because they trust you. So, trust the Lord always, because he is our Rock forever."
Isaiah 26:3-4

In repairing a relationship, it's essential to realize that no friendship is perfect, no marriage is perfect, no person is perfect. With the resolve that you are going to make a relationship work, you can develop peace treaties of love and tolerance and harmony to transform a difficult situation into something beautiful.

THE SPIRIT HELPS US

The Spirit helps us with our weakness. We do not know how to pray as we should. But the Spirit himself speaks to God for us, even begs God for us with deep feelings that words cannot explain.
Romans 8:26

Father, we invite you to work in our hearts today. This day would be nothing without your spirit – convicting, convincing, encouraging, and helping us. We can do nothing on our own and so we ask you for your help in all we do.

CARRY MY BURDEN

*"I will give rest and strength to those
who are weak and tired."*
Jeremiah 31:25

Can you say to Jesus, "This burden's too
heavy for me. I want you to be my co-
worker. I want you to carry this burden
with me. I cannot do it any longer." He
says if you will come to him, if you'll allow him to carry that burden with you,
his promise is that you will receive rest.

THE ROCK OF MY PROTECTION

But the Lord is my defender; my
God is the rock of my protection.
Psalm 94:22

If you're facing a problem, perhaps what you need to do is just simply calm down, settle down, and start thinking. Don't try to douse it, don't try to rationalize it. Don't try to escape it. Just think it through, with God's help.

A COVENANT OF LOVE

"You keep your loving promise and lead the people you have saved. With your strength you will guide them to your holy place."
Exodus 15:13

Don't think that God always has goose bumps and happy feelings toward his people. That same God is the God who once wondered if he should have ever made this thing called the human race. But it's the same God who assures us that "you are my people and I will be your God." It's not based on feelings or perfection; it's based on a covenant of love.

THE PRIVILEGE OF SERVING

God began doing a good work in you, and I am sure he will continue it until it is finished when Jesus Christ comes again.
Philippians 1:6

Father, we pray for your servants who devote their lives to sharing your Good News throughout the world. We ask your blessing upon them and we pray that you strengthen them. And Father, lift up our eyes and help us to be aware of people we've never seen, languages we've never heard. We are grateful for the privilege of serving you.

Expand Our Vision

*"There is joy in the presence of
the angels of God when one
sinner changes his heart and life."*
Luke 15:10

Expand our vision, Father, and help us see
the world as you see it. Touch us so that
we would grieve over the global sin that
causes you to grieve, that we would weep
over the world hunger that causes you to
weep. Give us the eyes of Christ, that we
may see the world as you see it and care
for it as you do.

COHEIRS OF
ETERNAL SALVATION

*Make every effort to give yourself to God
as the kind of person he will accept. Be a
worker who is not ashamed and who
uses the true teaching in the right way.*
2 Timothy 2:15

Your home is simply a means to take you
to a greater end – a heavenly end. Working together as coheirs of eternal salvation
is the foundation for the home.

LOOK IN YOUR OWN HEART

Light shines on those who do right;
joy belongs to those who are honest.
Psalm 97:11

When we look in our own heart – honestly, doggedly, prayerfully before God – and realize that perhaps we haven't done as much as we could to make a relationship work, immediately animosity begins to be diluted with tenderness, and understanding begins to surface.

LOVE YOUR NEIGHBOR

*"'Love the Lord your God with all
your heart, all your soul, all your
strength, and all your mind.' Also,
'Love your neighbor as you love yourself.'"*
Luke 10:27

Servanthood is seen when you realize that communication falls to the speaker and not to the hearer. When you're communicating with someone, it's your responsibility to see that the listener understands. Put yourself in the shoes of the other person, speak their language, live their hurts, feel their fears, and help them.

To That Cross We Turn

*He is able to protect what he has
trusted me with until that day.*
2 Timothy 1:12

Father, in the midst of hectic schedules,
we come to you. What was supposed to
give us more time seems to take more time
to run. What was supposed to free us up
seems to imprison us. And, Lord, there are
times when the only stability in the world
is the Cross of Christ. So to that Cross we
turn, praying that you would give us the
courage to do only what needs to be done
in your eyes, through your power.

GOD DWELLING WITHIN YOU

Know that the Lord is God. He made us, and we belong to him; we are his people, the sheep he tends.
Psalm 100:3

Dwell on the fact that God lives within you. Think about the power that gives you life. The realization that God is dwelling within you may change the places you want to go and the things you want to do today.

Sanctification – A Lifelong Process

*All things are worth nothing
compared with the greatness of
knowing Christ Jesus my Lord. Because
of him, I have lost all those things, and
now I know they are worthless trash.*
Philippians 3:8

Salvation is the process that's done, that's secure, that no one can take away from you. Sanctification is the lifelong process of being changed from one degree of glory to the next, growing in Christ, putting away the old, taking on the new.

A VICTOR IN GOD'S VICTORY

Fight the good fight of faith, grabbing hold of the life that continues forever. You were called to have that life when you confessed the good confession before many witnesses.
1 Timothy 6:12

Do you know why you should feel grateful? You are a part of God's plan, you are touched by God's tenderness, and you are a victor in God's victory. What greater blessing could there be?

NOVEMBER

NOVEMBER 1

AN ACT OF WORSHIP

This is my prayer for you: that your
love will grow more and more; that
you will have knowledge and understanding
with your love ... that you will do
many good things with the help of
Christ to bring glory and praise to God.
Philippians 1:9, 11

When you take food to the poor, that's an act of worship. When you give a word of kindness to someone who needs it, that's an act of worship. When you write someone a letter to encourage them or sit down and open your Bible with someone to teach them, that's an act of worship.

A Reason To Be Alive

But our homeland is in heaven, and
we are waiting for our Savior, the Lord
Jesus Christ, to come from heaven.
By his power to rule all things, he
will change our simple bodies and
make them like his own glorious body.
Philippians 3:20-21

You belong to God's eternal dream. Now you may not feel motivated, you may not feel like you have a reason for living, but you must renew your mind with the immovable fact that you are part of a commissioned people – you have a reason to be alive.

Your Sins Are Covered

*All who believe in Jesus will be forgiven
of their sins through Jesus' name.*
Acts 10:43

There are some facts that will never change.
One fact is that you are forgiven. If you
are in Christ, when he sees you, your sins
are covered – he doesn't see them. He sees
you better than you see yourself. And that
is a glorious fact of your life.

NOVEMBER 4

MORE LIKE JESUS

Lord, show your love to us
as we put our hope in you.
Psalm 33:22

God, give us strength as we try to be more like Jesus in our homes. We ask you to keep the evil one away from us; keep us close. Let our homes be testimonies of your love for us, that when people see our homes, they would see how you have loved the world.

MAKE AN ETERNAL DIFFERENCE

Also pray for us that God will give us an opportunity to tell people his message. Pray that we can preach the secret that God has made known about Christ.
Colossians 4:3

We are here on earth to be God's people. We are here to show others the same God who came to be a friend to the earth – that's our task. Maybe today you will meet someone who really needs a friend – and you can fill that need. Maybe you can make an eternal difference in that person's life, just because you choose to be friendly today.

Forgive And Let Go

Those who love your teachings will find true peace, and nothing will defeat them.
Psalm 119:165

The God who is willing to forgive you has already forgiven you much more than you could ever forgive anyone else. The best thing you can do to bring peace to your life is to forgive the mistakes of others. I'm not saying to justify their mistakes; I'm saying forgive them and let go.

NOVEMBER 7

POWERFUL INDWELLING

"But Lord, you are our father.
We are like clay, and you are the
potter; your hands made us all."
Isaiah 64:8

Father, we invite your assistance and guidance and powerful indwelling, because we do not have the strength to be transformed into your likeness and not be conformed to this world. May we understand more of what it means to say, "It is well with my soul."

Pursuit Of Things

"It is worth nothing for them to have the whole world if they lose their souls. They could never pay enough to buy back their souls."
Matthew 16:26

Being busy is not a sin. Jesus was busy. Paul was busy. Peter was busy. Nothing of significance is achieved without effort and hard work and weariness. That, in and of itself, is not a sin. But being busy in an endless pursuit of *things* that leave us empty and hollow and broken inside – that cannot be pleasing to God.

NOVEMBER 9

THAT SAME POWER

"The Lord made the earth by his power.
He used his wisdom to build the world and
his understanding to stretch out the skies."
Jeremiah 51:15

The power that lives in God's children is the same power that was present at the Creation, calling into being this existence that we call the world. That same power was present, inspiring David, inspiring the prophets. That same power is alive today to convince you, convict you, equip you, and encourage you.

Our Bodies Become Temples

*Dear friends, we have these promises from
God, so we should make ourselves pure —
free from anything that makes body or soul
unclean. We should try to become holy in
the way we live, because we respect God.*
2 Corinthians 7:1

God has chosen to dwell in us, and our
bodies become much more than carcasses
carrying around flesh and bone. Our bodies
become temples in which God has chosen
to dwell.

NOVEMBER 11

Setting Us Free

Lord, you bless those who do what is right;
you protect them like a soldier's shield.
Psalm 5:12

Thank you, Father, for setting us free. May
we be spurred on by your love to do great
works, yet never substituting those works
for your great grace. May we always hear
your voice. Keep us free from our own
legalism, our own systems. Keep us amazed
and mesmerized by what you have done
for us.

HEAL THEIR WOUNDS

The Lord gives strength to his people;
the Lord blesses his people with peace.
Psalm 29:11

Father, I would pray a special prayer for those who have gone through divorce. Will you give them peace? Will you hold them in the palm of your hand and heal their wounds as only you can?

SEE HIS MERCY

The Lord is kind and shows mercy. He does not become angry quickly but is full of love.
Psalm 145:8

The first step in finding your place in God's plan is to see his mercy – instead of looking inside yourself, look up to him and reflect upon and understand his mercy. How great is the call of God!

ALL-WEEK-LONG WORSHIP

Come into his city with songs of thanks-giving and into his courtyards with songs of praise. Thank him and praise his name.
Psalm 100:4

Our biblical act of worship is not what we do on Sunday mornings in coats and ties, but our act of worship is a lifelong, seven-days-a-week process of placing ourselves upon an altar of sacrifice. Worship is living the principles of Christ in everything we do. You're worshiping God by what you do all week long.

GRACE

*Because he was full of grace
and truth, from him we all
received one gift after another.*
John 1:16

Grace is a pleasant surprise. Grace is a kind gesture. Grace is something you did not expect. It is something you certainly could never earn. But grace is something you'd never turn down.

Speak Up And Help The Hopeless

Speak up for those who cannot speak for themselves; defend the rights of all those who have nothing. Speak up and judge fairly, and defend the rights of the poor and the needy.
Proverbs 31:8-9

Jesus demonstrated his tenderness by helping those people forgotten by society: He helped the deaf, he helped the lepers, he helped the blind, he helped the crippled. This was how he proved that he was the Messiah: He had a different way of looking at people. He helped those who had no hope.

HARDENED HEARTS

Happy is the person whose sins are forgiven, whose wrongs are pardoned. Happy is the person whom the Lord does not consider guilty and in whom there is nothing false.
Psalm 32:1-2

Father, have mercy on our hardened hearts. Forgive us for being witnesses of your majesty and yet living like you did not exist. Teach us the meaning of repentance, Father.

HARMONY

"You have chosen to bless my family. Let it continue before you always. Lord, you have blessed my family, so it will always be blessed."
1 Chronicles 17:27

God's goal for your home is harmony. That means a family of individuals singing different notes, but with the same score of music, with the same goal.

I'M YOURS

"So I tell you, ask, and God will give to you. Search, and you will find. Knock, and the door will open for you."
Luke 11:9

Surrendering our life to Christ means going to him and saying, "I'm yours; use me however you want to." Once you've done this, you can begin to seek his will for your life.

FOCUSING ON THE FATHER

*"You do great and wonderful things, Lord
God Almighty. Everything the Lord does
is right and true, King of the nations."*
Revelation 15:3

In the midst of a busy life on the freeway of humanity, it seems that the faster we go, the emptier we become. When we're always in a hurry trying to get ahead, never taking time to pause and reflect, we sacrifice a lot to stay on top. Sometimes it takes hard decisions to bring our life under control and realign our priorities, focusing on the Father and letting everything else take a backseat.

NOVEMBER 21

HEAR MY PRAYER

*Answer me when I pray to you, my
God who does what is right. Make
things easier for me when I am in trouble.
Have mercy on me and hear my prayer.*
Psalm 4:1

God knows that we with our limited vision don't even know that for which we should pray. And we are praying for things right now that God knows would not be best for us. When we entrust our requests to him, we trust him to honor our prayers with holy judgment.

Unquenchable Love

The Lord doesn't become angry quickly, but he has great love. He forgives sin and law breaking.
Numbers 14:18

No matter what you do, no matter how far you fall, no matter how ugly you become, God has a relentless, undying, unfathomable, unquenchable love from which you cannot be separated. Ever!

IF YOU BELIEVE

*"If you believe, you will get anything
you ask for in prayer."*
Matthew 21:22

Parents, don't give up. It's not too late for the child who has brought only tears. Think of Jesus' parents; the mother who had to watch her son crucified saw her son raised from the dead. Though you may go to the grave wondering if your prayers will ever be answered, don't stop praying. God blesses faithfulness.

THINGS THAT NEVER SATISFY

*The person with understanding is
always looking for wisdom, but the
mind of a fool wanders everywhere.*
Proverbs 17:24

One source of man's weariness is the
pursuit of things that can never satisfy, but
which one of us has not been caught up in
that pursuit at some time in our life? Our
passions, possessions, and pride – these are
all *dead* things. When you try to get life
out of dead things, the result is only
weariness and dissatisfaction.

FAITH AND FAMILY

Lord, your love reaches to the heavens, your loyalty to the skies.
Psalm 36:5

As an air force general addressed five or six hundred military personnel at his retirement party, he said that the priorities of his life were first, his faith and second, his family. "As I entered the military, I knew that someday I would leave it. If I made the military my whole life, what would happen when this day came? But with my life centered on faith and family, I still have everything!"

The True Voice
Of Jesus Christ

"Depend on the Lord and his strength; always go to him for help."
1 Chronicles 16:11

Father, help us to say no to the world and yes to you. Help us to hear the true voice of Jesus Christ amid the voices of pressure and success and power. We don't really know how, unless you come and help us.

THE GIFTS YOU HAVE

God never changes his mind
about the people he calls and
the things he gives them.
Romans 11:29

I look at some gifted people – some God-given gifted people – and oftentimes I wish I could do what they do. But God doesn't want us to feel guilty. Use the gifts you have, because God never calls us to do more than that for which he has equipped us.

Examine Your Own Heart

*Patience and encouragement
come from God. And I pray that
God will help you all agree with
each other the way Christ Jesus wants.*
Romans 15:5

When you have a relationship in need of repair, the first key to improvement is to examine your own heart. Look at your own heart – remember who you are and who God called you to be. Did the Father call you to be angry? To be bitter? Or did he call you to be loving and forgiving?

GOD'S POWER

Your love is wonderful. By your power you save those who trust you from their enemies. Protect me as you would protect your own eye. Hide me under the shadow of your wings.
Psalm 17:7-8

Simply because you can't put your hands around something doesn't mean it's not there. In fact, those things that are most precious to us are the things that are invisible, aren't they? Love, tenderness, happiness, air, feelings, emotions – those things we cannot touch, but they are very real. And so it is with God's power: It may not be touchable, but it's real and it's obtainable.

NOVEMBER 30

REMAIN TRUE

Now we hope for the blessings God has for his children. These blessings, which cannot be destroyed or be spoiled or lose their beauty, are kept in heaven for you.
1 Peter 1:4

It's not easy to hear the voice of God when popular opinion tells you it's okay to be immoral, or when your friends cheat on their income tax. But if you remain true to what you know to be right and godly, God says you will be blessed.

DECEMBER

SET FREE BY YOUR GRACE

My grace is enough for you. When you are weak, my power is made perfect in you.
2 Corinthians 12:9

Father, will you please help us to forgive others? Help us to forgive the one who has hurt us the most. And help us to forgive ourselves – even as you have forgiven us – that we might not live burdened and shackled by yesterday's failures, but that we might live set free by your grace.

DECEMBER 2

ALL BASED ON LOVE

The Son of God has come and has given us understanding so that we can know the True One. And our lives are in the True One and in his Son, Jesus Christ. He is the true God and the eternal life.
1 John 5:20

Father, we look at your plan and it's all based on love, not on our performance, and we pray that you'd help us to understand that. To be captivated by your love. To be overwhelmed by your grace. To come home to you in that beautiful path that you've already carved out for us.

DECEMBER 3

LIVE IN PEACE

Live in peace with each other.
1 Thessalonians 5:13

That "peace that passes understanding" cannot be obtained if we sacrifice valuable relationships at the expense of fleeting gratifications.

DECEMBER 4

CONCENTRATE ON THE NECESSARY

*My child, listen and accept what
I say. Then you will have a long life.
I am guiding you in the way of
wisdom, and I am leading you on the
right path. Nothing will hold you
back; you will not be overwhelmed.*
Proverbs 4:10-12

If you want to bring under control a fast-paced life-style, you must eliminate the unnecessary; if you want to be where God wants you to be, you must concentrate on the necessary.

DECEMBER 5

FULL OF DISCIPLINE

The love of money causes all kinds of evil.
1 Timothy 6:10

Here's something that's important to remember: Forget tomorrow's material pleasures because giving in to them can spoil your long-term devotion to your family with the burden of needless debt. You need to be dogged, determined, and full of discipline to avoid this trap.

DECEMBER 6

THAT KIND OF FRIEND

*A friend loves you all the time, and
a brother helps in time of trouble.*
Proverbs 17:17

A good lesson on the faithfulness of a friend, is in the story of the paralytic whose friends took him to be healed by Jesus. When they saw crowds of people hanging outside the windows and door, it would have been easy for those friends to turn back. Instead, they cut a hole in the roof and lowered their sick friend down to Jesus. What loyalty of friendship! Are you that kind of friend?

REWARD FOR FAITHFULNESS

Dear friends, now we are children
of God, and we have not yet been
shown what we will be in the future.
But we know that when Christ comes
again, we will be like him, because
we will see him as he really is.
1 John 3:2

Any difficulties we face in life are short-lived; all rewards are eternal. A divine inheritance will be our reward for faithfulness to our heavenly father. Our faithfulness to the Father is something we should renew daily – a priority for beginning our day.

HEAR OUR QUESTIONS

"Lord, I know that a person's life doesn't really belong to him. No one can control his own life. Lord, correct me, but be fair."
Jeremiah 10:23-24

We pray, O Father, that in the hours when we find ourselves in the dungeons of doubt, that you would hear our questions. Forgive us for demanding that you answer our questions like we want them to be answered. Forgive us for having certain expectations that we think you should meet.

DECEMBER 9

YOUR SPIRITUAL GUIDE

This God is our God forever and ever.
He will guide us from now on.
Psalm 48:14

You don't need anybody to intervene between you and God. The Scriptures are available to every person, and the gospel is simple; we can understand it. You need only God to be your spiritual guide.

DESTINATION: HEAVEN

Jesus, the One who says these things are true, says, "Yes, I am coming soon." Amen. Come, Lord Jesus!
Revelation 22:20

Good will triumph. God will win. The fate of our enemy, Satan, is sealed. With God as our guide, our destination is heaven. Hallelujah!

SET FREE

"Love the Lord your God with all your heart, all your soul, all your mind, and all your strength."
Mark 12:30

God wants to emancipate his people; he wants to set them free. He wants his people to be not slaves but sons. He wants them governed not by law but by love.

TOTALLY DEPENDENT ON HIM

It does not belong to us, Lord.
The glory belongs to you because
of your love and loyalty.
Psalm 115:1

I believe that many of us go through life sucking on pacifiers. Oh, we don't see them because they're in our bank. Or they're parked in our garage. Or we live in them. Jesus wants us to be totally dependent on him so that we might fortify our faith.

The Right Perspective

God, I will thank you forever for what you have done. With those who worship you, I will trust you because you are good.
Psalm 52:9

Gratitude comes from having the right perspective. It's being able to look at what you have and being thankful for that, rather than longing for what you don't have.

WHEN THE GOING GETS TOUGH

The Lord God is like a sun and shield; the Lord gives us kindness and honor. He does not hold back anything good from those whose lives are innocent.
Psalm 84:11

If God has been with you this far, he's not going to leave you when you're in troubled times. If your faith has brought you this far, don't throw your faith out when the going gets tough.

DIFFERENT FROM US?

*God looked down from heaven on
all people to see if anyone was wise, if
anyone was looking to God for help.*
Psalm 53:2

In one of the greatest testimonies to the
authenticity of Scripture, the Word of God
doesn't avoid showing the weaknesses of
man; it doesn't cover up the unpleasant, it
doesn't hide the dents in the armor. In an
honest look at humanity, we read that
Abraham doubted, that Moses lost his
temper, that Peter denied his Lord. These
chosen men of God – were they so different
from us?

HONEST QUESTIONS

*"Remember that I commanded you
to be strong and brave. Don't be
afraid, because the Lord your God
will be with you everywhere you go."*
Joshua 1:9

God never turns his back on those who ask honest questions. He never did in the Old Testament; he never did in the New Testament. So if you are asking honest questions of God, he will not turn away from you.

DECEMBER 17

OPENING OUR HEARTS

Lord, every morning you hear my voice. Every morning, I tell you what I need, and I wait for your answer.
Psalm 5:3

Father, we confess that sometimes prayer isn't very easy. We don't see you, and we don't see you hearing our words, but we have so many experiences in our own lives where prayers have been answered by faith that we continue coming before you, opening our hearts to you through prayer.

Your Repentant Heart

Without faith no one can please God.
Anyone who comes to God must believe
that he is real and that he rewards
those who truly want to find him.
Hebrews 11:6

Have you ever avoided the embrace of God in order to receive the acceptance of your peers? Have you, then, experienced the genuine turning of your repentant heart back to the Father and felt his consuming acceptance?

SMALL TROUBLES

*We have small troubles for a
while now, but they are helping us
gain an eternal glory that is
much greater than the troubles.*
2 Corinthians 4:17

Father, thank you for carrying us when we struggle. We're grateful that you don't turn your back when we're in trouble. Help us not to minimize our struggles, and yet at the same time, help us recognize that any struggle we have is small in comparison to the great God we serve.

DECEMBER 20

THE RIGHT THING TO DO

*Only the Lord gives wisdom; he gives
knowledge and understanding ... Then you
will understand what is honest and fair
and what is the good and right thing to do.*
Proverbs 2:6, 9

Never let your decisions be made on the
basis of the blowings of the winds of opin-
ions and popularity.

THAT CANDLE OF HOPE

I find rest in God; only he gives me hope.
Psalm 62:5

If hope dies, we begin to die, don't we? As long as we can keep that candle of hope lit, as long as we can keep that spark of possibility afire, then we can stay strong.

A MESSAGE OF LIFE

*Praise be to the God and Father
of our Lord Jesus Christ. In God's
great mercy he has caused us to be
born again into a living hope, because
Jesus Christ rose from the dead.*
1 Peter 1:3

The life of Jesus Christ is a message of hope, a message of mercy, a message of life in a dark world.

For The Sake Of This Special Child

*"The Lord has blessed you and
is with you ... Don't be afraid,
Mary; God has shown you his grace."*
Luke 1:28, 30

Maybe God chose Mary because he knew she would be the one to fortify herself, to be embroiled in inner turmoil for the sake of this special child. It wasn't easy raising the Son of God. And Mary was the one who would sit at his bedside at night and look at this one who didn't look like a king and wonder, *What am I supposed to do?*

THE PATTERN FOR PEACE

Agree with one another, and
live in peace. Then the God of
love and peace will be with you.
2 Corinthians 13:11

Those who call themselves followers of God
need to deal with the issue of peace
seriously: There will be peace on earth only
when there is peace between man and God.
After all, the pattern for peace comes from
heaven itself – in Jesus, who reconciled
earth to God through the Cross.

DECEMBER 25

A STAR IN THE DARKNESS

Christ had no sin, but God made him become sin so that in Christ we could become right with God.
2 Corinthians 5:21

A wise man saw a star in the east and exclaimed to his companions, "There's a big star – there's a beautiful star in the darkness!" How symbolic for what Jesus was – he was a star in the midst of darkness. For though he was in the midst of sinful people, he did not engage in their sins, and though he was offered a taste of sin, he never took it.

A Personal Invitation

Lord, tell me your ways. Show me how to live. Guide me in your truth, and teach me, my God, my Savior. I trust you all day long.
Psalm 25:4-5

When Jesus says, "Come to me," he doesn't say come to religion, come to a system, or come to a certain doctrine. This is a very personal invitation to a God, an invitation to a Savior.

MISTAKES TURNED
INTO OPPORTUNITIES

*I can do all things through Christ,
because he gives me strength.*
Philippians 4:13

God can take our mistakes and turn them
into opportunities. He's shown us, over and
over, through the lives of people like David,
Paul, Peter. He can do the same for us.

WHERE TO FIND REST

*I said to myself, "Relax, because
the Lord takes care of you."*
Psalm 116:7

Do you know where to find rest? Where you find a clean conscience? Where you find the ability to sleep at night and live with yourself? By living in the pleasure of the Father who made you.

SAFE PASSAGE

*Those who go to God Most High
for safety will be protected by the
Almighty. I will say to the Lord, "You are
my place and my safety and protection.
You are my God and I trust you."*
Psalm 91:1-2

Listen to the counsel of God, re-establish
your roots, and pray. This is the only way
to achieve safe passage through a crisis in
your life.

WE'RE NOT ALONE

*The Lord is my strength and
shield. I trust him, and he helps me.*
Psalm 28:7

God did not leave you as an orphan. He
says he will be with you always. All of us
could use some more strength – who isn't
trying to tackle an attitude or put away a
bad habit or overcome guilt? We can't see
the power, but it's real – we're not alone.

THE SPECIAL GIFT OF GRACE

*Christ gave each of us the special gift
of grace, showing how generous he is.*
Ephesians 4:7

The more we are loved by God, the more we are going to love. The more we are forgiven, the more we're willing to forgive. The more we're treated with patience, the more we are willing to treat others with patience. These are all extensions of that gift of grace.